The Social Dynamics of Web 2.0

Within only a few years, Facebook, Wikipedia, Twitter, YouTube and other social media have become an intimate part of everyday life. Web 2.0, the collective term for all forms of interactive online communication, is characterised by the overwhelming ability of users to collaboratively create content. The implications of Web 2.0 have become a central focus for interdisciplinary social science research.

This book comprehensively addresses the profound impact of Web 2.0 on contemporary society and its dynamics in a multiplicity of fields. The chapters, authored by world-leading experts, vividly demonstrate that Web 2.0 is a dynamic basis for collective action and an unlimited source of societal destabilisation and revolutionary change, for better or for worse. Various aspects of the radical transformative potential of Web 2.0 are imaginatively and critically discussed in the analytical context of quantitative approaches, qualitative works and case studies. This book provides key insights into the wide-reaching implications of recent technological developments, casting new light into an area which may potentially contribute to a more peaceful and sustainable future.

This book was originally published as a special issue of *Contemporary Social Science: Journal of the Academy of Social Sciences*.

Charalambos Tsekeris is Visitor at the Hellenic Naval Staff and Command College and Senior Researcher at the Lab of Virtual Reality, Internet Research & E-Learning, Panteion University, Athens, Greece.

Ioannis Katerelos is a Social Psychologist and Professor of Social Research Methods at Panteion University, Athens, Greece.

Contemporary Issues in Social Science
Series editor: David Canter, University of Huddersfield, UK

Contemporary Social Science, the journal of the **Academy of Social Sciences**, is an interdisciplinary, cross-national journal which provides a forum for disseminating and enhancing theoretical, empirical and/or pragmatic research across the social sciences and related disciplines. Reflecting the objectives of the Academy of Social Sciences, it emphasises the publication of work that engages with issues of major public interest and concern across the world, and highlights the implications of that work for policy and professional practice.

The *Contemporary Issues in Social Science* book series contains the journal's most cutting-edge special issues. Leading scholars compile thematic collections of articles that are linked to the broad intellectual concerns of *Contemporary Social Science,* and as such these special issues are an important contribution to the work of the journal. The series editor works closely with the guest editor(s) of each special issue to ensure they meet the journal's high standards. The main aim of publishing these special issues as a series of books is to allow a wider audience of both scholars and students from across multiple disciplines to engage with the work of *Contemporary Social Science* and the Academy of Social Sciences.

Titles in the series:

Crowds in the 21st Century
Perspectives from contemporary social science
Edited by John Drury and Clifford Stott

Biologising the Social Sciences
Challenging Darwinian and Neuroscience Explanations
Edited by David Canter and David Turner

The Social Dynamics of Web 2.0
Interdisciplinary Perspectives
Edited by Charalambos Tsekeris and Ioannis Katerelos

The Social Dynamics of Web 2.0
Interdisciplinary Perspectives

Edited by
Charalambos Tsekeris and Ioannis Katerelos

First published 2014
by Routledge
2 Park Square, Milton Park, Abingdon, Oxfordshire OX14 4RN

and by Routledge
711 Third Avenue, New York, NY 10017, USA

First issued in paperback 2015

Routledge is an imprint of the Taylor & Francis Group, an informa business

© 2014 Academy of Social Sciences

All rights reserved. No part of this book may be reprinted or reproduced or utilised in any form or by any electronic, mechanical, or other means, now known or hereafter invented, including photocopying and recording, or in any information storage or retrieval system, without permission in writing from the publishers.

Trademark notice: Product or corporate names may be trademarks or registered trademarks, and are used only for identification and explanation without intent to infringe.

British Library Cataloguing in Publication Data
A catalogue record for this book is available from the British Library

ISBN 13: 978-1-138-92293-8 (pbk)
ISBN 13: 978-0-415-73353-3 (hbk)

Typeset in Garamond
by Taylor & Francis Books

Publisher's Note
The publisher accepts responsibility for any inconsistencies that may have arisen during the conversion of this book from journal articles to book chapters, namely the possible inclusion of journal terminology.

Disclaimer
Every effort has been made to contact copyright holders for their permission to reprint material in this book. The publishers would be grateful to hear from any copyright holder who is not here acknowledged and will undertake to rectify any errors or omissions in future editions of this book.

Contents

Citation Information   vii
Notes on Contributors   ix

Foreword
David Canter   xi

1. Web 2.0, complex networks and social dynamics
   Charalambos Tsekeris and Ioannis Katerelos   1

2. Information sampling and linking: *Reality Hunger* and the digital knowledge commons
   Brooke J. Wonders, Frederic I. Solop and Nancy A. Wonders   15

3. An illustrated framework for the analysis of Web2.0 interactivity
   Peter Mechant   31

4. Networks for citizen consultation and citizen sourcing of expertise
   Cristobal Cobo   51

5. The political economy of information production in the Social Web: chances for reflection on our institutional design
   Vasilis Kostakis   73

6. Social intermediaries and the location of agency: a conceptual reconfiguration of social network sites
   Martin Berg   89

7. Musical tastes in the Web 2.0: the importance of network dynamics
   Kostas Kasaras, George Michael Klimis and Martha Michailidou   103

Index   119

Citation Information

The chapters in this book were originally published in *Contemporary Social Science: Journal of the Academy of Social Sciences*, volume 7, issue 3 (November 2012). When citing this material, please use the original page numbering for each article, as follows:

Chapter 1
Web 2.0, complex networks and social dynamics
Charalambos Tsekeris and Ioannis Katerelos
Contemporary Social Science: Journal of the Academy of Social Sciences,
volume 7, issue 3 (November 2012) pp. 233–246

Chapter 2
Information sampling and linking: Reality Hunger *and the digital knowledge commons*
Brooke J. Wonders, Frederic I. Solop and Nancy A. Wonders
Contemporary Social Science: Journal of the Academy of Social Sciences,
volume 7, issue 3 (November 2012) pp. 247–262

Chapter 3
An illustrated framework for the analysis of Web2.0 interactivity
Peter Mechant
Contemporary Social Science: Journal of the Academy of Social Sciences,
volume 7, issue 3 (November 2012) pp. 263–282

Chapter 4
Networks for citizen consultation and citizen sourcing of expertise
Cristobal Cobo
Contemporary Social Science: Journal of the Academy of Social Sciences,
volume 7, issue 3 (November 2012) pp. 283–304

Chapter 5
The political economy of information production in the Social Web: chances for reflection on our institutional design
Vasilis Kostakis
Contemporary Social Science: Journal of the Academy of Social Sciences,
volume 7, issue 3 (November 2012) pp. 305–320

CITATION INFORMATION

Chapter 6
Social intermediaries and the location of agency: a conceptual reconfiguration of social network sites
Martin Berg
Contemporary Social Science: Journal of the Academy of Social Sciences, volume 7, issue 3 (November 2012) pp. 321–334

Chapter 7
Musical tastes in the Web 2.0: the importance of network dynamics
Kostas Kasaras, George Michael Klimis and Martha Michailidou
Contemporary Social Science: Journal of the Academy of Social Sciences, volume 7, issue 3 (November 2012) pp. 335–349

Please direct any queries you may have about the citations to clsuk.permissions@cengage.com

Notes on Contributors

Martin Berg is Senior Lecturer in Sociology at Halmstad University, Sweden, but is currently appointed as Senior Researcher at the digital agency Good Old where he leads a three-year research project investigating online sociability and social network sites with financial support from *The Bank of Sweden Tercentenary Foundation*. He received his PhD from Lund University, Sweden, in 2008. His award winning doctoral thesis 'The fabricated self: self-reflexive gender play and queer social psychology' established a theoretical framework based on the tensions between Judith Butler and George H. Mead while using an analysis of self-presentations and diaries of cross-dressers on the web-community qruiser.com as an empirical foundation.

Cristobal Cobo has a PhD in Information and Communication Sciences and is a Research Fellow at the Oxford Internet Institute, University of Oxford, UK.

Kostas Kasaras holds a degree in Political Science and Public Administration from the University of Athens, Greece, and an MA in Sociology of Contemporary Culture from the University of York, UK. He is currently a doctoral candidate at the Department of Communication, Media and Culture, Panteion University, Athens, Greece. His first published work is 'Music in the Age of Free Distribution' which can be viewed at FirstMonday.org.

Ioannis Katerelos studied Sciences of Education at the University of Marseille-Aix en Provence, France, where he obtained his Doctoral Degree in Social Psychology. He is Professor of Social Research Methods at the Department of Psychology, Panteion University of Social and Political Sciences, Athens, Greece. His academic interests involve research methods, with particular emphasis on social dynamics, agent-based modelling, social network analysis, and Chaos/Complexity Theory in the Social Sciences.

George Michael Klimis, is currently Assistant Professor at Panteion University, and Adjunct Professor at the Open University, both in Greece. He has published extensively in academic journals such as the *European Management Journal*, *British Journal of Management*, *European Journal of Communication*, *New Media and Society* and others. One of his papers was also awarded the 'Most Innovative Paper' Award by the British Academy of Management in 1998.

NOTES ON CONTRIBUTORS

Vasilis Kostakis is a Research Fellow at Tallinn University of Technology, Estonia, and the P2P Foundation. Currently he investigates the political economy of the conjunction of Commons-based peer production with desktop manufacturing capabilities.

Peter Mechant has a PhD in Communication Sciences. He works at the research group for Media and ICT (IBBT-MICT-UGent) at Ghent University, Belgium. He has been mainly involved in research projects focusing on e-culture, Web2.0 and online communities. He has published in journals such as *Observatorio*, *International Journal of Web-based Communities* and the *International Journal of Electronic Governance*. He has co-authored papers in journals such as the *Journal of Computer-mediated Communication* and *Cyberpsychology, Behaviour, and Social Networking*.

Martha Michailidou is a Lecturer in the Department of Communications, Media and Culture at Panteion University, Athens, Greece. Her research interests include methods of media and communications research, sociology of media and culture, the production of culture in contemporary creative industries, governmentality and the relations between popular culture, cultural consumption and the government of populations.

Frederic I. Solop is Professor of Politics and International Affairs at Northern Arizona University, USA. His areas of expertise include digital democracy, elections and social movements, public opinion analysis and research methodology.

Charalambos Tsekeris graduated with Distinction from Brunel University (Department of Human Sciences), UK, and earned his doctoral degree in Reflexivity from Panteion University, Athens, Greece. He is a Visitor at the Hellenic Naval Staff and Command College and Senior Researcher at the Lab of Virtual Reality, Internet Research and E-Learning, Department of Psychology, Panteion University of Social and Political Sciences, Athens, Greece. He has given numerous invited lectures, and written papers for scientific meetings and conferences. His research interests involve human complex systems, virtual communities and psychosocial studies.

Brooke J. Wonders is a PhD candidate in the Program for Writers at the University of Illinois at Chicago, USA. Her research interests include creative nonfiction, post-modern literature and trauma theory.

Nancy A. Wonders is a Sociologist and Professor of Criminology and Criminal Justice at Northern Arizona University, USA. Her scholarship focuses on globalization and borders, social inequality and the justice system, and the development of sustainable and just communities.

Foreword

It is often claimed that the Soviet Union was destroyed by information. Yet the Berlin Wall tumbled down before the internet and todays many means of access to information was available. It is also clear that the fires of more recent revolutions were fanned, further than was possible when the Iron Curtain melted, by the ability of ordinary people to utilize what are now known as social media to keep in contact with each other and be informed of what is happening. And with the exponential expansion, even over the last few months, of Web 2.0, the collective term for all forms of interactive online communication, it is important for social scientists to get a grip of the far reaching implications of these developments.

Although they've been in existence for only a few years, Facebook, Wikipedia, Twitter, YouTube and blogs have become an integrated part of people's lives. Yet these well-known interactive media are already been overtaken by thousands of others, such as MySpace, Digg, Stumbleupon, Linkedin, Flicker, QQ in China, VKontakte, Bibo, Skyrock, StudiVZ, Netlog, Tuenti, Baddu, Photoblog and many, many more. These are generating social and political consequences that are difficult to predict. In particular the change from becoming a source of information to becoming a major form of social interaction raises many important questions for social scientists.

Therefore this volume in the *Contemporary Issues in Social Science* series devoted to the Social Dynamics of Web 2.0, is very timely. Interestingly and importantly, the special issue has two Greeks as its editors: Charalambos Tsekeris and Ioannis Katerelos from Panteion University in Athens. They have included contributors from Ghent, Arizona, Tallinn and Halmstad in Sweden as well as the Oxford Internet Institute, showing this is an area of inevitably international significance. These international perspectives help us to understand how diverse the impacts are of Web 2.0. For example in the UK incitement to riot and rumours circulating the web have been a cause for concern that have led to court proceedings, whilst in places like Greece and Estonia, recently free from Totalitarian regimes, Web 2.0 is seen as a powerful democratising influence.

This divergence in attitudes to Web 2.0 is itself an illustration of how much we need to understand what is happening in virtual reality. Studies by social scientists are revealing the mind boggling complexity of Web 2.0 and the many different directions in which it is pulling. These directions can be distinguished in part by the ownership of the social media. Many are still propriety, owned by corporations that can use them for their own end. These tended to be the first wave of the interactive internet. The more recent developments put the content firmly in the hands of the consumers,

FOREWORD

notably blogs and all similar media such as YouTube. Consumers become pro-sumers, being both producers and consumers. And the research shows that the prospects for this expansion in social interaction, of changing what it means to be a citizen, becoming a digital citizen, should not be idealized. There is still a long way to go.

Nonetheless, despite the inevitable weaknesses of these new forms of social interaction, consideration of Web 2.0 by social scientists is throwing new light on the essence of being human. The conventional interpretation of the Darwinian imperative is that human beings are inevitably in competition, programmed to destroy each other in a fight for survival, which is barely masked by the flimsy patina of social conditioning. In line with these Darwinian ideas the current socio-economic assumption, that guide so many theories and policies, is that people are motivated entirely by self-interest. Government strategies may shape that egocentricity by the hidden manipulation of market forces, or modify it by the gloved metal of central government. Yet Web 2.0 is challenging that perspective on being human. It is showing a more optimistic way of conceptualizing human interaction, that it is possible to view people in a much better light and that this is probably more fruitful. Given appropriate means the social web presents a picture of cooperation – much more dominant than competition.

Hopefully the reflexive study of interpersonal interaction in Web 2.0 and beyond will facilitate the development of ever more fair minded, moral, transparent and, crucially, easy to use systems that will contribute to a peaceful and sustainable future. That is why this volume is such an important contribution to our understanding of *Contemporary Issues in Social Science.*

Professor David Canter
Editor, *Contemporary Social Science*

Web 2.0, complex networks and social dynamics

Charalambos Tsekeris and Ioannis Katerelos

Department of Psychology, Panteion University of Social and Political Sciences, Athens, Greece

With the aim of contextualising this special issue of *Contemporary Social Science*, a brief overview of the relationship between the Web 2.0 and social dynamics is presented. It is argued that the Web tends to destabilise the social structure, radically re-organising human culture, identities, and socialising. It also calls for reflexive reconsideration for many of the dual oppositions that have traditionally been worked with, such as public/private, virtual/real, consumption/production, and so on. This overview critically explores and evaluates the impact that the Web 2.0 is having on a wide range of social processes by turning its analytic focus on both theoretical and methodological advances. The latter refers to the demonstration of the exponential growth of political blogging in Greece, leading to a major change in information exchange, as well as to a computer simulation of both Web 1.0 and Web 2.0 networks. It is vividly shown that what mostly defines Web 2.0 and differentiates it from Web 1.0 is the explosion of user-generated content (a fundamental bottom-up process). This amazingly reinforces social dynamics and provides a stable flow of unpredictable creativity, innovation and adaptation.

Introduction

Over the last decade, the triumphal advent of Web 2.0, also known as the social Web, read/write Web, or wisdom Web, has rapidly triggered a huge mass of exciting developments and radical transformations, mainly characterised by a wide range of online contributory practices (such as 'blogs', 'tagging', 'feeds', 'commenting', 'rating', 'mashing up', 'making friends', and so on) and, in general, by the overwhelming ability of users to interact and collaboratively create content (see Tapscott & Williams, 2006). According to Tim O'Reilly's best known definition (Fuchs, 2011, p. 288):

> Web 2.0 is the network as platform, spanning all connected devices; Web 2.0 applications are those that make the most of the intrinsic advantages of that platform: delivering software as a continually-updated service that gets better the more people use it, consuming and remixing data from multiple sources, including individual users, while providing

their own data and services in a form that allows remixing by others, creating network effects through an 'architecture of participation', and going beyond the page metaphor of Web 1.0 to deliver rich user experiences.

In contrast to Web 1.0 (1993–2003), mostly involving commercial sites created (pre-structured) and controlled by distinct producers and passively used by separable consumers (online content changes little over time), the by and large more humanised internet of Web 2.0 (2004 onwards) is primarily defined by sites which are interactively produced, wholly (blogs) or in part (YouTube), by the consumer itself, who is not self-contained (atomised), but both autonomous and interdependent, that is, radically individualised.

In Web 2.0, more and more users continuously 'work', usually without any financial reward, in order to produce that which they consume (for example, they both produce and consume their profiles and networks on YouTube or Facebook). Given the ontological blurring of the hitherto sharp distinction between producer and consumer, it is clear that Web 2.0 gives rise to the concept of 'prosumption' or 'prosumer' culture (Ritzer & Jurgenson, 2010, p. 19):

> Web 2.0 is defined by the ability of users to produce content collaboratively, whereas most of what exists on Web 1.0 is provider-generated. It is on Web 2.0 that there has been a dramatic explosion in prosumption. It can be argued that Web 2.0 should be seen as crucial in the development of the 'means of prosumption'; Web 2.0 facilitates the implosion of production and consumption.

From this theoretical perspective, Wonders *et al.* (2012) maintain that, in the digital age, users are no longer merely consumers of information or knowledge; through online social networks, they are increasingly both producers and distributors of information, thus satisfying their own 'hunger to define reality'. Through the use of new media, ordinary people around the world are explicitly 'hungry for reality—a reality they help to create ... this new form of information construction is synergistically related to the development of Web 2.0 technology, which allows for easy access to huge swaths of information, extraction of information samples, information linking, and aggregating—and ultimately information production and redistribution' (Wonders *et al.*, 2012, this issue).

Wikipedia and social networking sites (SNS) like Facebook are essentially prosumption sites, where the analytic focus is on the actual quality of users' interactions and contributions. While the basic structure of these sites is relatively stable, the emergent output is largely uncertain, unregulated, and unpredictable, thus potentially surprising users every time they log in.

The output is also unquantifiable due to the vast diversity, speed and complexity of what is going on within Web 2.0. This complexity profoundly affects intersubjectivity and identity construction and affords individuals the 'freedom to define and construct themselves around ... alternative cultural forms, experiences, and practices' (Kahn & Kellner, 2003, p. 300). Web 2.0 continues to dynamically evolve, substantiating new orders of emergence, such as Web 3.0, pertaining to smart transactional services, and Web 4.0, giving rise to digital citizenship.

Developments in Web 2.0

Nowadays, it is customary to refer to Web 2.0 as ultra-complex networks exchanging or co-creating information and knowledge, ceaselessly re-constituting and re-shaping the social structure. In other words, common knowledge depicts the internet of Web 2.0 as the central power engine of social dynamics, repeatedly transmitting and organising human culture, creativity, identities, and socialising.

Methodologically, Web 2.0 triggered a data revolution and inspired rigorous data-driven approaches, sensitive to the dynamics of communication in virtual contexts. Large, persistent, and near real-time digital data sets (pertaining to user-generated content online) are now searchable and almost ubiquitous (Giglietto & Rossi, 2012, p. 26):

> Contemporary communications and social processes leave - both intentionally and unintentionally - a growing number of digital traces: personal communication shared in social network sites, family relationships declared on Facebook or political thoughts and opinions posted on Twitter are just the top of the iceberg of the dataset available to digital social researchers.

Computational, data-driven approaches potentially offer a huge capacity for looking at and modelling, in a both flexible and accurate way, surprising combinations of strong ties, weak ties, and structural holes that decisively transcend the well-defined modern order (once figured out by formal functional analysis). Web 2.0 also offers an ever increasing interconnectedness of system components through software, bringing together (or networking) people who know or do not know each other, directly and indirectly. This in turn produces increased, far from-equilibrium and highly unpredictable 'system' effects (Barabási, 2002).

These developments largely involve the emergence of a novel (rather post-human) species of community, the so-called virtual or online communities. Virtual communities, originally anticipated by J.C.R. Licklider and R.W. Taylor as early as 1968 (Licklider & Taylor, 1968), increasingly moved towards the 'vision of a citizen-designed, citizen-controlled worldwide communications network is a version of technological utopianism that could be called the vision of "the electronic agora"' (Rheingold, 1993, p. 14). This reflexively entails the innovative dynamical conception of *digital citizenship* as a fundamental capacity to actively engage and participate in society, economy, and politics *online*.

Recent findings also strongly emphasise the democratic or participatory potential of Web 2.0 platforms, such as Flickr and deviantART, but do carefully point to the effort and the work still needed to really fulfil this potential (Mechant, 2012). In his article, Mechant (2012) perceptively describes how Web 2.0 users deploy Flickr functional affordances to gain access to a virtual third place, where people gather, communicate and share with each other, as well as how deviantART actually act as a 'virtual community'.

However, Cobo (2012) illustrates that by no means can the mere inclusion of Web 2.0 platforms be theorised as a guarantee of citizen engagement and participation.

The use of social-media tools as a shortcut to strengthen citizen involvement can possibly generate unforeseen and unanticipated outcomes (Cobo, 2012, this issue):

> The adoption of *social-media tools* among public-service websites is not synonymous with citizen participation or transparency ... a complex network of components exists, including information availability, adequate social tools, social capital and digital literacy, each of which contributes to the creation of a climate that facilitates public participation.

We should also remain vigilant against the closed elements of the virtual worlds. Distinguishing between proprietary-based and Commons-based platforms, distinguished by the organisation of information production in each case, Kostakis (2012) points to the ambivalence of the social production which is taking place in Web 2.0. In that context, he comprehensively argues that these platforms 'exhibit both emancipatory and exploitative aspects, and the political struggle of online communities and users should be to foster the one over the other, strengthening the Commons sphere' (Kostakis, 2012, this issue).

Nevertheless, the dimension of social interaction is always fundamental. Within SNS, such as YouTube, MySpace, Facebook, Twitter, Digg, StumbleUpon, LinkedIn, Flickr, QQ (China), Vkontakte, Bebo, Skyrock, StudiVZ, Netlog, Tuenti, Badoo, and Fotolog, 'significant others' (i.e. people belonging to your personal network), one can be seen and scrutinised and they can see and scrutinise you too. According to Boyd and Ellison (2008), an SNS is a universal 'web based service that allows people to (1) construct a public or semi-public profile within a bounded system, (2) articulate a list of other users with whom they share a connection, and (3) view and traverse their list of connections and those made by others within the system'.

Research to date has focused on various aspects of online social networking, such as online relationships and online–offline connections, friendship and intimate relationships, profiles and self-presentation, privacy and surveillance, anonymity and trust, and so on. But since such research tends to locate the actor at quite different levels, suggesting a conceptual separation between individual-oriented and system-oriented agency, we prefer the term 'social intermediaries'—instead of 'SNS' (Berg, 2012).

This arguably provides a reflexive way to re-conceptualise SNS with respect to their functional position in the social, thus offering an important alternative to contemporary instrumental and institutional accounts (Berg, 2012, this issue):

> social intermediaries should not only be regarded as sites and applications that provide a means for individual pursuits or function as instruments for harvesting personal information but rather as distinct and somewhat independent entities. Understood in this way, social intermediaries enter the social situation as a third actor, while at the same time providing the infrastructural condition for that very situation [...] In this sense, such a conceptualisation of social intermediaries provides an opportunity to shift focus towards the social realm as such, which facilitates the establishment of an understanding that can be critically related to a larger theoretical whole.

Moreover, online networking requires new automated data extraction (data mining) techniques, transdisciplinary quantitative methods of rigorous analysis and robust empirical findings about the internal logic and organisation of internet-connected communities, where the real/corporeal (or physical), as we have hitherto known it, is dynamically reconfigured. For example, social networking websites freely give the unique, unprecedented chance to transdisciplinarily grasp 'the impact of a person's position in the network on everything from their tastes to their moods to their health, whereas Natural Language Processing offers increased capacity to organize and analyze the vast amounts of text from the Internet and other sources ... In short, a computational social science is emerging that leverages the capacity to collect and analyze data with an unprecedented breadth and depth and scale' (Lazer et al., 2009, p. 722).

This also involves new experimental designs for the careful investigation of online behaviour, such as the emergent forms of influence developing in cyberspace. Using several aspects of social networking analysis, Kasaras et al. (2012, this issue) opt for an experimental plan that seriously challenges 'the applicability of hierarchical models of influence developed during the course of the 20th century for the analysis of complex, and potentially horizontal, relations of influence which may be indigenous to the contemporary social networks developing in the ecology of the Web 2.0'.

In the same spirit, many scientists and scholars perceptively consider virtual communities and virtual worlds in general as adequately 'good environments in which to explore wider issues related to emerging technologies, such as intellectual property rights and the sociotechnical implications of online misbehavior', with the particular transdisciplinary aim of 'adjudicating between alternative theoretical propositions and thereby connecting the currently isolated schools of thought' (Bainbridge, 2007, pp. 474, 475).

Furthermore, special transdisciplinary requirements of distributed monitoring, permission-seeking, privacy, and encryption are of utmost importance. For the crucial reason that a 'single dramatic incident involving a breach of privacy could produce rules and statutes that stifle the nascent field of computational social science, a self-regulatory regime of procedures, technologies, and rules is needed that reduces this risk but preserves research potential' (Lazer et al., 2009, p. 722).

Online networks, like other contemporary techno-social systems, consist of 'large-scale physical infrastructures ... embedded in a dense web of communication and computing infrastructures whose dynamics and evolution are defined and driven by human behaviour' (Vespignani, 2009, p. 425). But human behaviour is mostly non-linear; it is characterised by a strong disproportionality between (changes to) the input and the outcome. In other words, a small cause often has large effects (see, e.g. Urry, 2005, p. 6). That is why online networks are chaotic systems: determinism is structurally coupled with the role of agency, contingency and unintended consequences (unpredictability).

The multiscale nature, diversity, and complexity of these networks are crucial features in better understanding them. Both methodological and epistemological advances in complex online networks are providing an integrated framework, without however achieving true predictive power of their behaviour. This particularly indicates that chaos, unpredictability, non-linearity, and indeterminacy, as significant constitutive features of the emergent virtual worlds, should always be placed at the centre of the analysis.

However, these features refer to an ultra-complex environment which almost seems irreducible to analytic interrogation: structures emerging from everyday interactive activities, within online life worlds, signify a wholly new (post)human condition, importantly enhanced by modern technology and its operative fusion with data, information, and knowledge.

The case of blogs

This fusion has rapidly taken on the dimensions of a daily social revolution. In the early years of the past decade, the terms 'weblogs', 'blogs', and 'blogging' were relatively unknown. Blogging is nowadays a very familiar practice in the Web 2.0 internet cultures and one of the most common forms of user-generated content; it is now almost a part of the cultural mainstream. Blogs (a compression of 'web log') can be roughly defined as emergent

> spaces where individuals, or groups, write for an online audience. These are often described as online diaries that users frequently update. The types of entries made vary quite considerably and are not always limited to the type of entries that you might expect to see in a diary. So for instance ... sociologists operating sociologically informed blogs where they discuss their work, academic conferences, recent publications, contemporary debates in the discipline and so on (Beer & Burrows, 2007, par. 2.2)

The huge, inexhaustible, and undiminishing power of blogging has almost conquered the static, homogenous, and one-sided logic of television and television coverage. For the first time in the history of human communication, dialogue is making listeners autonomous, individualised, and active, in a truly participative and democratic way.

Of course, up-to-date experience implies that the 'democratising effects' of blogs (or social networking platforms like Twitter) may also reduce the level of critical public discussion, rather than substantially elevating it, as well as absorb 'the accuracy that comes from reliance on experts' (Tenopir, 2007, p. 36). Ignorant mob attitudes and misinformation never go away, so that 'our collected information becomes infected by mistakes and fraud' (Keen, 2007, p. 65). We therefore need to permanently provoke and challenge Web 2.0's ideological embedment and false claims, often reinforced by powerful commercial interests and professional elites (Scholz, 2008).

But the qualitative complexity of online communication is crucial. In blogging, we observe lots of people communicating with lots of people and not just one to one (as, for example, with the telephone) or one person communicating with many (as with radio and television). Theoretically, a communication situation in which everyone talks to everyone would inevitably lead to an absolute stability of the system. But, in fact, many talk to many on the World Wide Web, continuously producing localities and causing a radical and non-linear transformation of the social structure (online and offline) (Tsekeris, 2009b).

The spontaneous emergence of the blogosphere reflexively turned the Web into something like a global brain, a kind of collective intelligence that uninterruptedly creates new knowledge and new social values (e.g. prosumption). The on-going interdependence of blogs and links increasingly enables human minds and virtual communities to fruitfully interconnect to each other in and through a self-expressive anonymous *thinking collective*, which is unified in its vast diversity and made possible through the fluid blogosphere (Tsekeris, 2008).

Actually, nothing is more social than the blogosphere itself—a self-evolving, ateleological and deterritorialised Deleuzian world, without ends, centres, and Gods. It creatively welcomes alterity (or non-identity) and generously gives a voice to almost everything. Everyone is potentially able to efficiently communicate and socialise with everyone (who is not physically present). This epochal non-linear process comprehensively allows humanity (as a whole) to reflexively communicate with itself.

Bloggers all over the world are now feeding mainstream print media, framing/deframing hot political debates, creating focal points, mobilising voters, and carrying out the crucial daily role of grassroots reporter and political fact-checker. Especially after 9/11, blogging (with its overwhelming what's new, what's hot, what's the buzz, what's important, what's on your mind etc) signifies an increasingly dominant form of *global technopolitics*. Well-respected political content providers, such as *The American Prospect*, *The New Republic*, the *New York Times*, and the *Wall Street Journal*, have repeatedly acknowledged and published many prominent bloggers (or even hired them as regular contributors) (Tsekeris, 2009c).

Everywhere in the world, blogs create active *citizen-journalists* and strongly empower (especially) young people with the demiurgic, democratic capacity to freely and openly express themselves, outside of the old, conventional and strictly hierarchical institutions prevalent in established political systems. During the last 10 years, in Greece, an exponential growth of political blogging has been witnessed, leading to a major change in information exchange; that is, a radical large-scale shift from traditional media (radio, television, newspapers) to a completely volatile scenery of decentralised and unbounded information spread.

In 2012, a simple web search, starting from four specific blogs and following the 'blog rolls' presented in each blog (terminated in a radius of 4, that is, repeating the process three times until a radius of 4), a technique akin to snowball sampling, eventually ended up with 13,158 nodes (blogs) with 30,583 links between them (Figure 1).

Simulating Web 1.0 vs. Web 2.0

In the extremely rapid and complex topology of Web 2.0, any 'top-down' control of information spread, opinion formation, and self-expression is difficult and undesirable. A predictable, pure/homogenous, and stable or motionless/inert social system does not exhibit any dynamic characteristics; it is therefore doomed to die (or dissipate). This would probably be 'a very hopeless, colourless, periodical, monotonous, dull and boring world: A completely grey social universe (*against human nature itself*)' (Tsekeris, 2010, p. 39).

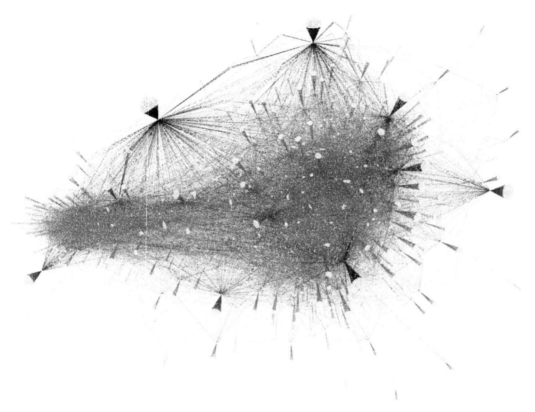

Figure 1. The blogosphere in Greece: 13,158 nodes (blogs) with 30,583 links between them (blog rolls) (This picture courtey of Ioannis Katerelos and George Michael Klimis, Athens Panteion University, Greece.)

An allegedly privileged way of illustrating social dynamics is agent-based (or multi-agent) computer simulations—that is, an innovative way of simulating social behaviour grounded on minimal rules, simplicity, and emergence. Axelrod (1997) comprehensively describes social simulations as a wholly new approach for social sciences and, beyond that, *as a third way of doing science.*

Radically different from induction or deduction, social simulations have the high ambition of presenting a new kind of thinking and, consequently, new and surprising findings (Epstein & Axtell, 1996; Friedkin, 1998). This kind of computational modelling can help to vividly show (in a bottom-up manner) the multiple effects of both social network macro-types and the micro-personalities of the social agents themselves.

We can therefore investigate the emergent consequences of local interactions for global structures and, at the same time, the holistic impact of global patterns upon local behaviours and individual personalities. In this experimental research setting, 'the social, (dis)order, (dis)organization and (mis)understanding reflexively come from chaos, heterogeneity, autopoiesis, agonist competition, irreducible diversity, mutual evolution and emergence' (Tsekeris, 2009a, p. 4041).

Specifically, the HESIOD model (Katerelos, 2012), seeking to systematically quantify social dynamics, uses two basic indexes: Lyapunov exponent (Sprott, 2003) and information entropy (Peitgen et al., 1992). The first measures the system's sensitivity to initial conditions, thus expressing the overall stability or instability of the system. The latter expresses the degree of self-organisation of the system, since less entropy entails more order and less chaos.

In particular, we experimentally designed and implemented two different social networks (of 100 agents each), and simulated their dynamics. In order to demonstrate the idiosyncratic dynamic effects of the Web 1.0 communication topology (a largely centrally conceived and controlled topology), we preferred to implement a 'star graph', which corresponds to an individual-based type of communication, in the sense that all agents are individually linked to a central one, in a complete absence of peer-to-peer interaction—that is, in a social-sharing vacuum.

As seen in Table 1, the average clustering coefficient, regarding such a type of communication network, equals zero (that is, no closed triad), although the diameter is relatively low and equals 2.

As far as Web 2.0 is concerned, we preferred to use a small-world network (see Strogatz, 2003), since relevant studies indicate that Web 2.0 exhibits small-world features (Barabási, 2002). As seen in Table 2, such network types present a relatively high average clustering coefficient, albeit low density.

Table 1. A Web 1.0 type of communication topology (star topology) and its structural properties (Authors' design)

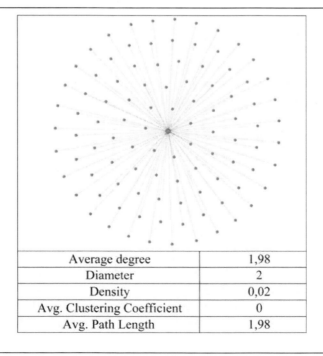

Average degree	1,98
Diameter	2
Density	0,02
Avg. Clustering Coefficient	0
Avg. Path Length	1,98

This signifies that, although the network is relatively scarce (that is, with only few direct connections between agents), the average path length remains at low values. In other words, within our artificial society, the agents live in a 'small world' governed by the rule of 'four degrees of separation', as described by Stanley Milgram's 'small-world effect' (Milgram, 1967).

Both networks were simulated, following the HESIOD model algorithm, in order to carefully investigate their dynamic characteristics. Figure 2 shows the results of simulating the 'Web 1.0 network', while Figure 3 does the same for the 'Web 2.0 network'.

The 'Web 1.0 network' case demonstrates that after a short period of turbulence (transient chaos), the system stagnates to a fixed point (flat lines). The Lyapunov exponent here equals to $\lambda = 0.001$, which clearly signifies that our Web 1.0 network-based system is mostly a top-down system; it is static and does not really fuel social dynamics.

Furthermore, this type of network exhibits a minimal entropy $I = 1.55$, which profoundly implies that such networks lead the artificial society to a stable, periodical, and highly ordered (self-organised) state, depriving it of any trace of dynamics.

Table 2. A Web 2.0 type of communication topology (small-world topology) and its structural properties (automatically generated by Gephi 0.8a)

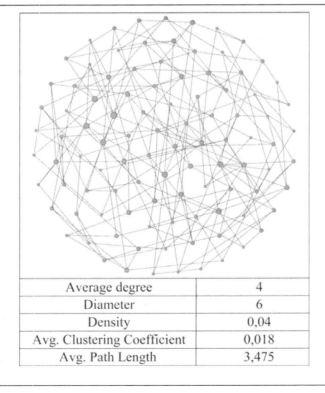

Average degree	4
Diameter	6
Density	0,04
Avg. Clustering Coefficient	0,018
Avg. Path Length	3,475

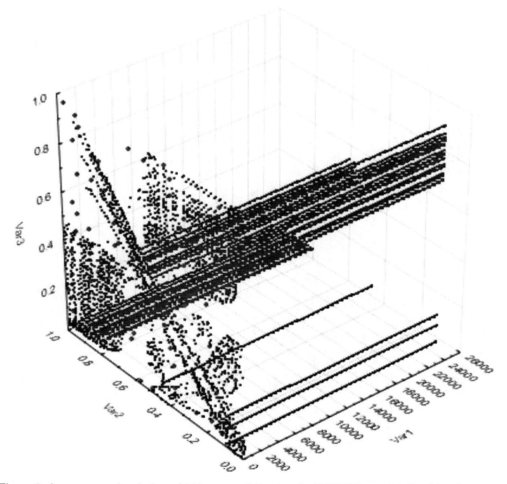

Figure 2. A computer simulation of 100 agents, following the HESIOD model algorithm for 25,000 iterations, corresponding to the Web 1.0 type of communication topology

In the 'Web 2.0 network' case, the experimental results are totally different. Here, the system is in permanent movement, without any steady state. Social groups become variously shaped, re-shaped, and de-shaped (dissolve), signifying that our system is constantly organising and dis-organising itself, never reaching a state of equilibrium. The Lyapunov exponent is now $\lambda = 0.150$, which denotes high sensitivity to initial conditions, as perceptively described by Edward Lorenz's 'butterfly effect' (Lorenz, 1963). Regarding information entropy, the system presents a value of $I = 3.99$, which means that it is moderately ordered.

Our Web 2.0 network-based system is a bottom-up system; it seems to actually trigger surprise and reinforce social dynamics (for better or for worse), as well as to rapidly produce social facts, thus introducing a stable flow of unpredictable creativity, innovation and adaptation.

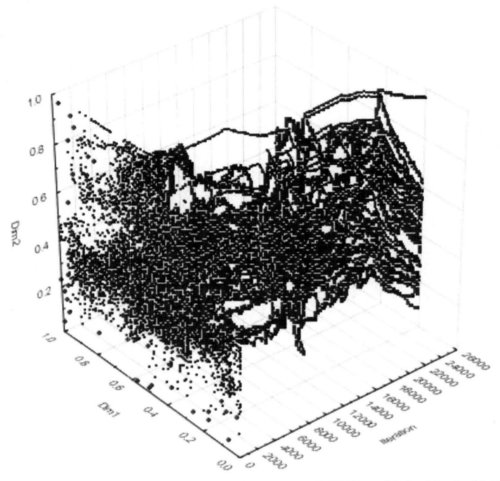

Figure 3. A computer simulation of 100 agents, following the HESIOD model algorithm for 25,000 iterations, corresponding to the Web 2.0 type of communication topology

Conclusion

Hence, the internet of Web 2.0 (paradigmatised by social media or online social networking platforms) can indeed be theorised as 'potentially disrupting, undermining or otherwise threatening the established way of doing things in society ... Whatever people are doing in [new] media, it clearly has become a threat to the establishment—even when it involves people expressing their unbridled embrace of the commodification of their deepest intimacies through commercial platforms for the public exchange of private information' (Deuze, 2012).

The Web 2.0 systematically inspires and strengthens individual and collective self-expression and improvisation, while rapidly fuels and spreads the flows of global activism and protest. Social media, as an innovative *general architecture of participation*, seem to effectively constitute new radical 'tools for rebellions that emerge from and question actual power relations and materialize themselves in spaces like Tahrir Square, Syntagma Square, Puerta del Sol, Plaça Catalunya, or Zuccotti Park' (Fuchs, 2012, p. 120).

This undoubtedly involves the dynamic interaction and intra-action between Web 2.0 and social life, or between the virtual and the real, which renders our contemporary reality (irreducibly) mutable and fragile as never before. However, more empirical and computational data-driven research is still needed to account for the social dynamics of Web 2.0, a transdisciplinary academic field that promises exciting intellectual developments.

Acknowledgements

We are grateful to David Canter for his continuous encouragement and support during the whole course of doing this special issue. We would also like to acknowledge all CSS's external reviewers for their valuable help in reviewing the paper submissions and bringing the articles to their current form.

References

Axelrod, R. (1997) Advancing the art of simulation in the social sciences, *Complexity*, 3(2), 16–22.
Bainbridge, W. S. (2007) The scientific research potential of virtual worlds, *Science*, 317, 472–476.
Barabási, A.-L. (2002) *Linked. The new science of networks* (Cambridge, MA, Perseus).
Beer, D. & Burrows, R. (2007) Sociology and, of and in Web 2.0: some initial considerations, *Sociological Research Online*, 12(5). Available online at: http://www.socresonline.org.uk/12/5/17.html (accessed 12 June 2012).
Berg, M. (2012) Social intermediaries and the location of agency. A conceptual reconfiguration of social network sites, *Contemporary Social Science*, 7(3), 321–333.
Boyd, D. & Ellison, N. (2008) Social network sites: definition, history and scholarship, *Journal of Computer-Mediated Communication*, 13(1), 210–230.
Cobo, C. (2012) Networks for citizen consultation and n sourcing of expertise: exploring innovations in the public sector, *Contemporary Social Science*, 7(3), 283–304.
Deuze, M. (2012) Media life is a threat to social order, *Culture Digitally//Examining Contemporary Cultural Production*, 26. Available online at: http://culturedigitally.org/2012/01/media-life-is-a-threat-to-social-order (accessed 22 June 2012).
Epstein, J. & Axtell, R. (1996) *Growing artificial societies* (Cambridge, MA, MIT Press).

Friedkin, N. (1998) *A structural theory of social influence* (Cambridge, Cambridge University Press).
Fuchs, C. (2011) Web 2.0 prosumption, and surveillance, *Surveillance & Society*, 8(3), 288–309.
Fuchs, C. (2012) New Marxian times! Reflections on the 4th ICTs and Society Conference 'Critique, Democracy and Philosophy in 21st Century Information Society. Towards critical theories of social media', *tripleC—Journal for a Global Sustainable Information Society*, 10(1), 114–121.
Giglietto, F. & Rossi, L. (2012) Ethics and interdisciplinarity in computational social science, *Methodological Innovations Online*, 7(1), 25–36.
Kahn, R. & Kellner, D. (2003) Internet subcultures and oppositional politics, in: D. Muggleton & R. Weinzierl (Eds) *The post-subcultures reader* (Oxford, Berg), 299–313.
Kasaras, K., Klimis, G. M. & Michailidou, M. (2012) Musical tastes in the Web 2.0: the importance of network dynamics, *Contemporary Social Science*, 7(3), 335–349.
Katerelos, I. (2012) *Chaos and Order in Social Systems. The HESIOD Model: Social Dynamics Simulations* (Athens, Papazisis Publications) [forthcoming, in Greek].
Keen, A. (2007) *Cult of the Amateur* (New York, Doubleday).
Kostakis, V. (2012) The political economy of information production in the social web: chances for reflection on our institutional design, *Contemporary Social Science*, 7(3), 305–319.
Lazer, D., Pentland, A., Adamic, L., Aral, S., Barabasi, A. L., Brewer, D. D., Christakis, N., Contractor, N., Fowler, J., Gutmann, M., Jebara, A., King, G., Macy, M., Roy, D. & Van Alstyne, M. (2009) Computational social science, *Science*, 323(5915), 721–723.
Licklider, J. C. R. & Taylor, R. W. (1968) The computer as a communication device, *Science & Technology*, 76(2), 21–31.
Lorenz, E. N. (1963) Deterministic nonperiodic flow, *Journal of Atmospheric Science*, 20(2), 130–141.
Mechant, P. (2012) An illustrated framework for the analysis of Web2.0 interactivity, *Contemporary Social Science*, 7(3), 263–281.
Milgram, S. (1967) The small world problem, *Psychology Today*, 2(1), 60–67.
Peitgen, H.-O., Jurgens, H. & Saupe, D. (1992) *Chaos and fractals: new frontiers of science* (New York, Springer-Verlag).
Rheingold, H. (1993) *The virtual community: homesteading on the electronic frontier* (Reading, MA, Addison-Wesley).
Ritzer, G. & Jurgenson, N. (2010) Production, consumption, prosumption: the nature of capitalism in the age of the digital prosumer, *Journal of Consumer Culture*, 10(1), 13–36.
Scholz, T. (2008) Market ideology and the myths of Web 2.0, *First Monday*, 13(3). Available online at: http://firstmonday.org/htbin/cgiwrap/bin/ojs/index.php/fm/article/view/2138/1945 (accessed 10 August 2012).
Sprott, J. C. (2003) *Chaos and time-series analysis* (Oxford, Oxford University Press).
Strogatz, S. (2003) *Sync: how order emerges from chaos in the universe, nature and daily life* (New York, Hyperion).
Tapscott, D. & Williams, A. D. (2006) *Wikinomics: how mass collaboration changes everything* (London, Penguin).
Tenopir, C. (2007) Web 2.0: our cultural downfall? *Library Journal*, 132(20), 36.
Tsekeris, C. (2008) Thoughts on the nature of the virtual, *Ubiquity*, 9(28). Available online at: http://ubiquity.acm.org/article.cfm?id=1399626 (accessed 11 June 2012).
Tsekeris, C. (2009a) Advances in understanding human complex systems, *Australian Journal of Basic and Applied Sciences*, 3(4), 4040–4045.
Tsekeris, C. (2009b) Blogs and Society, *Intellectum*, 6(1), 97–102.
Tsekeris, C. (2009c) Blogging as revolutionary politics, *Research Journal of Social Sciences*, 4(2), 51–54.
Tsekeris, C. (2010) Chaos and unpredictability in social thought: general considerations and perspectives, *Sociologija. Mintis ir veiksmas*, 27(2), 34–47.
Urry, J. (2005) The complexity turn, *Theory, Culture and Society*, 22(5), 1–14.
Vespignani, A. (2009) Predicting the behavior of techno-social systems, *Science*, 325(5939), 425–428.
Wonders, B. J., Solop, F. I. & Wonders, N. A. (2012) Information sampling and linking: reality hunger and the digital knowledge commons, *Contemporary Social Science*, 7(3).

Information sampling and linking: *Reality Hunger* and the digital knowledge commons

Brooke J. Wonders[a], Frederic I. Solop[b] and Nancy A. Wonders[c]

[a]Department of English, University of Illinois, Chicago, IL, USA; [b]Politics & International Affairs, Northern Arizona University, Flagstaff, AZ, USA; [c]Criminology and Criminal Justice, Northern Arizona University, Flagstaff, AZ, USA

This article weaves together insights from the social sciences and humanities to explore the link between Web 2.0 technology, information diffusion, and what we describe as a 'hunger for reality'. Using David Shield's book *Reality Hunger* as both a critical muse and analytic lens, we explore linkages between form and meaning in the digital age. We suggest that Shields' central argument in *Reality Hunger* accurately reflects the way new information technologies have altered information production, distribution, and meaning. As a result of opportunities created by Web 2.0 technology, information today is increasingly 'sampled', rather than digested in whole. Information consumption comes in bits and bytes, fragmented and disconnected from original sources; it is repurposed in ways that increasingly valorise creativity over content, social networks over corporations, and collective knowledge over private intellectual property. In this article, we explore the social consequences of this new reality. In particular, we argue that individuals are no longer merely consumers of information; through social networks, they are increasingly both producers and distributors of information in the digital age, satisfying their own hunger to define reality. Through the use of Web 2.0 technology, ordinary people around the world are creating a new digital knowledge commons. We explore the implications of this new knowledge commons for the future and suggest reasons that new forms of reality hunger are likely to emerge.

Introduction

1. How shall we re-open mystery in our times? To emerge from under the shadow of inevitability, it seems important to bring back the passions and the stakes of global connection. Instead of inscribing structures of self-fulfilment, we might immerse ourselves in the drama of uncertainty.

2. The rapid proliferation of global computer-based networks and digitization of a broad array of economic and political activities enabling them to circulate in these networks raise questions about the effectiveness of current framings for state authority and democratic participation.
3. My own ability to enter this history is that of ethnographer—a listener and a teller of tales... In this project, I have used ethnographic fragments to interrupt stories of a unified and successful regime of global self-management.
4. What I want to do is take the banality of nonfiction (the literalness of facts, truth, reality), turn that banality inside out, and thereby make nonfiction a staging area for the investigation of any claim of facts and truth, an extremely rich theatre for investigating the most serious epistemological questions.
5. These questions can be explored by focusing on how digitization has enabled the strengthening of older non-state actors and spaces and the formation of novel ones capable of engaging the competence, scope, and exclusivity of state authority.
6. We desire 'a healthy and strong global critical public sphere capable and checking and correcting corruption of the state at every level'... 'alas, such a vision is pure and idealistic speculation'.
7. Facts quicken, multiply, change shape, elude us, and bombard our lives with increasingly suspicious promises.
8. Never again will a single story be told as if it were the only one.[1]

Perhaps the introduction to this article feels unusual... disconcerting, disconnected, yet provocative. These numbered segments do not sound like a unified voice; some of the segments may even sound contradictory, and while one could imagine a sustained narrative connecting them, it is a subtextual narrative that binds them together. This subtextual narrative requires the active involvement and participation of the reader. If contextual clues, including the article title, do not give it away, the numbered sections correspond to quotations cobbled together from contemporary works of literary non-fiction, political theory and literary theory.

The framework used to introduce this article is taken directly from David Shields's book, *Reality Hunger: A Manifesto* (2010). In this book, Shields aggregates over 600 fragments of writing from a broad swathe of critical thinkers to produce an account of the kind of reality he thinks the world is hungry for. Shields argues that today, what we think of as 'real information' is nothing more than aggregated information: the information we ingest is little more than a collection of bits and pieces appropriated from a wide range of sources. It is, in one sense, fragmentary and individuated and, in another sense, collective in its reliance on history and the relationality of meaning-making. In Shields' view, we all hunger for reality—yet, as he illuminates with his text, reality is creatively produced, historically situated, relational and, ultimately, illusive.

This article weaves together insights from the social sciences and humanities to explore linkages between Web 2.0 technology, information diffusion, and this hunger for reality. We use Shields' work as a both a critical muse and analytic lens to explore linkages between form and meaning in the digital age. Using an inductive approach, we suggest that Shields' central argument in *Reality Hunger* accurately reflects the way information technologies have altered information production and distribution. As we examine in this article, the opportunities created by Web 2.0 technology have transformed information in a fundamental way—information is increasingly 'sampled', rather than digested in whole. Information consumption comes in bits and bytes, fragmented and disconnected from original sources. As we will discuss, it is then repurposed in ways that increasingly valorise creativity over content, social networks over corporations, and collective knowledge over privately constrained intellectual property. In this article, we also explore the social consequences of this new reality. In particular, we argue that individuals are no longer merely consumers of information; through social networks, they are increasingly both producers and distributors of information. In this way, Web 2.0 technology allows ordinary people around the world the power to contribute to a new digital knowledge commons. We explore the implications of this new knowledge commons for the future and suggest reasons that new forms of reality hunger are likely to emerge.

Form and meaning: the hunger for reality

David Shields' *Reality Hunger* challenges popular conceptions of literary form within the world of creative nonfiction and has sparked an important debate about the relationship between creativity and appropriation of the work of others. In essence, Shields redefines plagiarism as a legitimate aesthetic choice rather than indefensible intellectual laziness. He justifies certain types of plagiarism (namely pastiche), arguing that artists have historically borrowed from one another as they take their place within respective canons. Artists should embrace this process, according to Shields, rather than mystify or deny an important component of the creative process.

According to Morrison's (2010) review of *Reality Hunger*: 'the book's premise is that "reality can't be copyrighted" and that we all have (or ought to have) ownership of each other's words'. Shields' intentional use of others' words without attribution is a hallmark of the text. As Morrison further notes: 'True, Shields has been forced to list his citations in small-print footnotes at the back of the book. But he invites readers to remove these with a razor blade, and in the main text we can't tell whether it's him or someone else talking'.

Another dimension of Shields' exploration of the boundaries between form and meaning involves a blurring of distinction between fiction and nonfiction. In *Reality Hunger*, Shields takes on the popular genre of memoir by questioning the fundamental assumption that authors have the capacity to tell an audience facts about their lives. The lines between nonfiction and fiction are blurred when history becomes filtered through memory and the human mind. Responding to the 2010 confrontation between Oprah Winfrey and author James Frey over the authenticity of information included in the memoir *A Million Little Pieces* (2005), Shields (2010, p. 43) declares in *Reality Hunger* that 'I'm disappointed not that Frey is a liar but that he isn't a better one. He should have said, *Everyone who writes about himself is a liar*'. His work emphasises that the value of information content is a function of a given subject position.

In our view, Shields' manifesto resonates because it arrives at a time when digital technology is giving citizens unprecedented access to information content. Those with access to Web 2.0 technologies now have a virtually unbounded capacity to produce and distribute content online to a very large network of readers. A revolution of form, synergistically linked to digital innovation, is redefining content and meaning in the modern world. Rather than simply being the passive recipients of information produced by a small number of large media conglomerates, today people digest smaller portions of information produced by a wide variety of sources. Further, users blend in their own comments on selected readings and distribute content they deem important to a network of social media users, thus enabling new kinds of participation in social and political life. How did we arrive at this new reality?

Web 2.0 and the information revolution

Web 1.0 technology was revolutionary, in large part, because it made a huge volume of information available to all Internet users, and it offered consumers a centralised repository of constantly updated information. At the same time, Web 1.0 technology remained rather analogous to traditional communication formats, including newspapers, television and radio, since all are fundamentally premised upon a one-dimensional flow of communication. In one-dimensional communications, information producers deliver content to information consumers who remain passive recipients.

The advent of Web 2.0 technology was not just a technological revolution; it was also a profound communication and information revolution. Web 2.0 technology enables information consumers to themselves become information producers and content distributors, and to actively interact with other information producers within the context of user communities (Mackay, 2010). Meaning is now created within socially networked environments. Social news aggregators such as *Digg* and *Reddit*, for example, allow anyone to add news links to these sites. Site users vote for the best stories and the collective wisdom of users helps prioritise the value and relative positionality of news content. Mobile application *Flipbook* goes so far as to present information from favourite social media sites in an easily digestible, personalised magazine format.

Digital technology makes it possible for large volumes of information to be stored in easily searchable formats. As a result, more information is readily accessible to today's 'information consumer' working within the digital environment. Automatic news aggregators such as *Yahoo! News* and *Google News*, and mobile applications such as *Fluent News* and *News360*, collect news content from multiple sources and instantaneously provide an overwhelming amount of news to the information consumer. Beyond simply assembling the news stories in categorised lists, news aggregator programs allow users to enter personal search terms and create tailored lists. Some services go beyond this level of service to analyse viewer behaviour and interests, and to individualise the presentation of information (e.g. the mobile application *Zite*) (Pariser, 2011).

Other information aggregators like *Google Reader* allow easy and instantaneous access to a variety of content, including blog posts. *Technorati* aggregates content from about 1.3 million blogs.[2] Other types of digital aggregators store video information (e.g. *YouTube*) and pictures (e.g. *Flickr, Picasa, Shutterfly, Instagram*), much of which has been created by ordinary people in the course of ordinary daily life. All of this digital content is easily referenced using a web browser of choice (e.g. *Chrome, Safari, FireFox, Explorer*). At a practical level, all of these formats permit individual users to decide what information is worth viewing—to customise their information consumption by mashing together information in creative ways—to sample information rather than to engage it holistically. Information from any of these sites can be copied, distributed, and commented upon in one's personal networks via *Facebook* or *Twitter*, for example. A wealth of information can be easily appropriated and repurposed. We explore these processes further in the next section.

Information sampling and linking

David Shields makes a provocative argument in favour of information sampling during the digital age. The concept of 'sampling' involves taking short bits of information from source material and repurposing the information so as to integrate it into newly created content. Sampling itself is not a new concept; it existed in an analogue world. Since the 1970s, many musical tunes appropriated beats, drum rolls, or guitar riffs from earlier songs and integrated these music samples into original creations (Goodwin, 1988; Ponte, 2006). The process of repurposing others' original creations is even more common today, as digital technologies make it easy for any young person with a computer to extract a few bars from a song and use the material elsewhere (Boyle, 2010). In the digital world, the process of sampling and appropriation extends beyond the world of music to include the integration of individual photographs and snippets of video into mash-ups of images, or taking information from news sources such as a national newspaper, a government agency or a non-profit organization and integrating it into a *Facebook* or *Twitter* post.

In the digital world, information sampling has become commonplace and can be found in many forms of information distribution. As Menzies (2005, p. 41) notes:

> In this hypermedia zone of flows, everything is fast and fleeting. Everything is fungible, too: mixing and mashing music is the new trend in culture; cutting and pasting the new trend in production, downloading is the new trend in identity.

Yet for some, particularly those born and raised within the analogue world, sampling is suspect; it represents a form of plagiarism or intellectual property theft. In January 2011, National Public Radio produced a segment on 'Talk of the Nation' dedicated to better understanding the implications of sampling in the music industry. Paralleling the issues Shields grapples with, NPR pondered: 'Is sampling theft, or is copyright law making creativity a crime?'[3]

The work of Shields' urges us to re-politicise the concept of plagiarism using a critical lens. As noted in Jonathan Lethem's 'The Ecstasy of Influence', a work which uses pastiche in a manner similar to Shields:

> The kernel, the soul—let us go further and say the substance, the bulk, the actual and valuable material of all human utterances—is plagiarism. For substantially all ideas are

secondhand, consciously and unconsciously drawn from a million outside sources, and daily used by the garnerer with a pride and satisfaction born of the superstition that he originated them; whereas there is not a rag of originality about them anywhere except the little discoloration they get from his mental and moral caliber and his temperament, and which is revealed in characteristics of phrasing. Old and new make the warp and woof of every moment. There is no thread that is not a twist of these two strands. (Lethem, 2007)

The very concept of 'plagiarism' is rooted in a nineteenth-century understanding of the primacy of private property and capital (Boyle, 2010). The idea that original content is proprietary and ought be copyrighted and protected from use by others led to the private enclosure of much knowledge that had previously been part of an intellectual commons. This nineteenth-century ethos is being fundamentally challenged in the twenty-first century by digital technology. Today, people with access to the Internet have unprecedented access to news, information, and commentary, and digital space permits a certain amount of power for ordinary people to determine how free information will be:

> The meteoric rise of open-source platforms, with examples such as Linux, Apache, Mozilla, and Wikipedia, is eroding the rationale for costly and exclusionary information. As activity migrates to the open-access and collaboration model, the case for accessibility is strengthened. On a mass scale, individuals are collaborating and making their contributions freely available to others. (Schor, 2010, p. 150)

Importantly, as Schor notes above, ordinary citizens are no longer simply consumers of information; they have increasingly become information producers and distributors. In addition, there has been a trend within virtual environments toward open sharing that is diametrically opposed to the idea of information as private property. Sassen (2007, p. 328) further reinforces this point:

> For instance, in Open Source networks much meaning is derived from the fact that practioners contest a dominant economic-legal system centred on protections of private property.... Participants become active subjects in a process that extends beyond their individual work and produces a culture.

Using Shields' manifesto as a defence of the blogger ethos of linking, we believe it is important to consider how this new culture and new forms of content production and distribution—blogs, vlogs, photo-sharing sites, social networks and news aggregators—change the way that meaning gets constructed in society. In our view, Shields' manifesto would also defend the digital ethos of 'linking', or embedding references to the work of others (e.g. music, video, pictures, written content or personal commentary) within original posts. Such information mosaics de-centre information ownership and the authority of the corporate media and, instead, place a value on individual perspectives, creativity and, importantly, on relationships and social networks.

At a descriptive level, the processes of sampling and linking create a mappable and networked web of relationships. A consumer of these otherwise discrete bits of information moves from site to site via hyperlink, while also making intellectual links of his or her own. Sampling and linking can be employed to create a book like Shields', or employed in the clever work of German artist Maria Fischer, whose physical manifestation of linking via colour-coded threads running through a printed text was an

Internet sensation in early 2011.[4] Or, to use a more common example, information sampling and linking allows more than 800 million users of Facebook the ability to create a personalised and, yet, deeply networked page.

Information sampling is easy to achieve using the Internet. After typing a few keys on the computer keyboard, one can read the canon of Victorian literature (Cohen, 2010) or news stories from the *New York Times*, the *Washington Post*, and practically every other news publication throughout the developed world. One can access information from independent sources, from a best friend in another country, or a sibling who lives across town. According to a recent report by Pew Research Center (2011), television now only barely eclipses the Internet for the attention of people who regularly digest news information (50%). And, importantly, more people are relying on the Internet for their news (46%) than on newspapers (40%).

In addition, with the advent of Web 2.0 technology, people are able to actively engage with news content by performing keyword searches and selectively reading stories about subjects of interest, choosing stories that resonate with their values and sharing stories and information fragments with members within their social networks. Thus, while information consumers are still reading news from established sources of content, they are now also relying on information provided by members of their social networks—friends, family members, colleagues, acquaintances and others. With Web 2.0, social networks have a significantly increased capacity to collectively define what is important to know and understand. Through the Internet, as in real life, social networks play a primary role in filtering and ordering the importance of information (Watts, 2003). Social networks help determine which stories, blog entries, podcasts, pictures, videos and events have legitimacy and value.

In the contemporary world of online knowledge construction, the text fragment does similar work to the hyperlink, in that knowledge is made via juxtaposition and aggregation. As a given link's popularity increases and is shared, its value as collective knowledge increases, if not its truth-value. In this way, those with access to new technologies play an integral role in defining what information is of value and what information should be reproduced and disseminated, shaping reality in the process. What are the consequences of this transformation for knowledge production and social life?

The new digital knowledge commons

Because of Web 2.0 technology, ordinary people are now playing an important role in information production and distribution. In the process, those with access to digital technologies are helping to forge a new 'digital knowledge commons'. This knowledge commons is decentralised, collaborative, and nonproprietary and has significant potential for shaping social and political life. Along with other scholars who are drawing attention to digital space as a powerful new global commons (Sassen, 2007; McKibben, 2008, 2011; Schor, 2010), we argue that the digital knowledge commons is potentially a powerful site for new forms of public participation and civic engagement.

Anyone with access to the Internet can post original information or share and comment on information collected elsewhere (AllTechnoblog, 2010). As Schor (2010, p. 150) emphasises, 'on a mass scale, individuals are collaborating and making their contributions freely available to others'. Bonds of community are forged as people actively interact with 'friends' and 'fans' using services such as *Facebook*, and with 'followers' using services such as *Twitter*. It is the sense of community that engages and empowers people, pulls people in, and holds their attention over time. Web 2.0 reaffirms a sense of personal power by encouraging people to be 'knowledge producers': to influence the worldview of others, to hear what others have to say, and to be moved to think about the world in new ways.[5]

Thus, social media networks are taking on the role of identifying what is important to know about the world around us. When individuals visit their personal *Facebook* page and see news stories posted by 'friends' and subsequent commentary added still by other 'friends', they assign greater importance to the information than if the story was accessed through the mainstream media. This is what it means to participate in a knowledge commons. Within the new digital knowledge commons, the rules that define what is important and what is not important are structured by personal bonds of trust and interdependence, rather than by impersonal corporate entities or unknown forces external to personal communities of interest.

It is important to emphasise that social networks are at the heart of this new form of knowledge production and distribution. The real power of Web 2.0 technology for political and social life may well be that on-line, interactive social networks allow for the expression of a wide variety of viewpoints while also reassuring individuals that their contributions play a valuable role in the building of new knowledge, discourses and communities. To the extent that this fosters a sense of personal and political efficacy, we suspect that digital engagements may well have implications far beyond digital space.

The potential for the creation of a new democratic discourse using Web 2.0 technology is enormous. Internet users now act as information DJs, scanning the availability of a broad array of information content, sampling from the population of information, adding in original content and creating coherent or (sometimes) incoherent narratives: social, political and cultural. Truth-value, then, is created in the spaces between cleverly juxtaposed snippets of information. The original source of the information often carries less weight than knowing which member of a personal network is forwarding, and thereby creatively repurposing, the information. In this way, digital space tends to shift legitimacy and authority away from the corporate world and nation-states and toward community and affiliation-based social networks.

As social network theory suggests, active information retrieval and dissemination within social networks transforms individuals and their relationships to others (Milgram, 1967; Putnam, 2011). Information flow and content sharing between social network members permits individuals to shift positionality from being passive, recipients of knowledge to active agents influencing the worldview of others. Participating in the flow of information, network members experience an increasing density of bonds within the network and the growth of social capital over time (Putnam, 2001). In this manner, individuals benefit from the distribution of sampled information by trusted network members and, reciprocally, become active agents promoting healthy democratic positionality within their personal network of relationships.

By providing a sense of the current scale of information sharing, we hope to further emphasise the importance of this dynamic—and of our argument. Early in 2011, *Facebook* indicated that 'more than 30 billion pieces of content (web links, news stories, blog posts, notes, photo albums, etc.) (were being) shared each month' by *Facebook* users.[6] At the same time, *Facebook* is huge with more than 800 million active members—indeed, if it were a country it would be the third largest (only China and India have more people)![7] And *Facebook* is only one platform that allows for linking, sampling, commenting on and repurposing of information. *AddThis*, an information-sharing site, works with 300 services. This company suggests that 44% of all information content shared occurs on *Facebook*.[8] This puts the volume of content shared on *AddThis* closer to 70 billion pieces of information and growing. *Addtoany*, another information sharing site, suggests that approximately 24% of all information content shared on the Internet is shared through *Facebook*.[9] If this is correct and 75% of information sharing takes place through other applications, then information sharing actually involves closer to 120 billion pieces of content per month.

However one looks at the statistics, the reality is that a huge number of people are participating in digital social network communities today (Barabasi, 2002; Watts, 2003), sharing links and sampled pieces of information, distributing original content and commenting on the posts of others and creating an aggregated worldview and 'digital knowledge commons' from the snippets of content shared by members of social network communities. How are we to understand the nature and extent of the digital commons?

Researching new realities

Given the important role of sampling and linking within the digital commons, the paucity of social science research on the topic is rather striking. Surprisingly, a search of JStore and EBSCO Host using the keywords 'content sharing', '*Facebook*' and 'Internet news' demonstrates that virtually no academic articles have considered the implications of these new distribution networks for information content and meaning production (however, see Boyd & Ellison, 2007, for a discussion of the importance of social network sites). Yet, these new forms are revolutionising communication and information by allowing people around the world to sample news content broadly and to repeat the words of others without reference to the original news source.

We believe that future research could deepen our understanding of the linkage between social networks and information dissemination. Research on the nature and extent of information sharing could help us to better assess the production of social capital through networks grounded in Web 2.0 technology, as well as the impact of the digital commons on social networks, social relationships and democratic life. Such research projects must be necessarily ambitious given the size of the virtual world, but already some computer scientists are developing algorithms that would permit large-scale investigation of this complex new knowledge-scape (Weber & Monge, 2011). And while some research on information distribution within online organisational networks exists (Schumate & Dewitt, 2008; Schumate & Lipp, 2008), few social science researchers have focused on individuals as information producers and distributors.

In conducting research, it is important to emphasise that it is the interactive and two-dimensional nature of Web 2.0 technology that has heightened the primacy of social networks as a major source of information content. The concept of social networks implies that information distributed within our networks is by default considered to be valuable and important, and that it will resonate with the interests of people within the social network (Putnam, 2001). While it is beyond the scope of this paper to fully explore the implications of network analysis, future research might productively focus on how information travels within social networks forged on the Internet, the volume of information being exchanged, the quality of this information, the extent to which this information increasingly reflects a global rather than local perspective of world events and the level of trust associated with information received from within the environment of social media networks.[10] As noted previously, while some have begun to develop the complex approaches that would allow for measurement of the impact of the Internet on information distribution (Weber & Monge, 2011), research on ordinary citizens as information producers and distributers is virtually nonexistent (but see the work of Finen et al. (2008) for an example of research on blogs). Yet, as Vergeer and Hermans (2008, p. 37) suggest, it is possible to employ a mixed methods approach, involving network analysis, content analysis and longitudinal analysis to better understand the new knowledge commons. They argue that the 'value of using a combination of research methods simultaneously is that it does justice to the complex object of study because a more in-depth and triangulated measurement of political communications can be established'.

Although primary research is thus far lacking, it is critical to consider how new forms of information production and diffusion will shape the future. What are some of the broader implications of this new reality?

New realities—new kinds of hunger

Web 2.0 has changed information production and distribution in ways that are likely to be enduring; in this section, we explore several implications of this trend including its impact on community, democracy and global networking and globalisation.

We believe that content sharing across the web will continue to grow in value and importance as younger generations of 'digital natives' replace older generations of computer users who are more sceptical of sharing information with their social networks using a digital platform. There is much empirical evidence to suggest this replacement of users is already taking place (Andarson & Rainie, 2010) and the volume of information being shared is increasing rapidly.

We further suggest that heightened democratic control over the distribution and creation of information is a positive development; in our opinion, the growth of a new digital knowledge commons promises to foster greater democratic participation in the body politic and can foster the construction of new forms of community. The last few decades have seen an incredible concentration of power within the media industry; fewer and fewer corporations control news outlets of every form (Bagdikian, 2004; Parenti, 2010). And it is still true that corporate news producers control the resources needed to hire reporters, deploy reporters in the field, and maintain sophisticated Internet sites for information distribution. At the same time, because of the Internet, information consumers are not as dependent upon these corporate sources as they once were.

It is no surprise to hear that the mainstream media is suffering from a loss of monopoly over the production of news content. Newspapers are losing subscribers, television audiences are disbursed across an increasingly larger number of cable and satellite channels, and locally programmed radio stations are becoming harder to find. A recent U.S. Federal Communications Commission report documents a 25% decline in staffing of daily newspapers since 2001 and laments the loss of quality local reporting (Waldman, 2011). Because digital technologies make it possible for people to sample stories, ideas, and information from a wider range of sources than ever before, our worldviews are less dependent upon corporate interests and increasingly reliant on information prioritised and distributed by members of our social networks. In this way, Web 2.0 has helped to create an information revolution characterised by more democratic control over the production and distribution of information content.

It may be tautological to say, but the relationship between trust and information sharing within communities is directly linked to the building of community. Community is both a foundation of social networks and a result of social networking and information sharing. Trust builds in communities over time and fuels the growth and importance of communities in shaping individual behaviour. This process of trust-building infuses information content with a depth of meaning beyond what would otherwise be true if one simply read an item of news content on a news aggregator. In this time of declining trust of public officials and news sources, the trust that is developing within online social networks may motivate the next generation of technology users to become 'self-educators' and to produce and share information critical to future political and social engagement. The 'Arab Spring' protests that swept throughout the Middle East and northern Africa in the spring of 2011 provide a striking example of the power of online networks for social change. It is also possible that the digital engagement being evidenced by this generation can be marshalled into greater political involvement if governments create avenues for civic engagement accessible through digital platforms—further heightening 'digital democracy' (Solop, 2001; de Zúñiga et al., 2010). We already know that participation using the Internet is different than off-line political participation (Jensen et al., 2007), but whether online discussion and sharing 'lead to more political participation and empowerment of peripheral groups, requires further empirical investigation' (Vergeer & Hermans, 2008, p. 52).

The growing strength of social networks on the Internet bodes well for the development of new forms of 'community'. While many high profile scholars have lamented the decline of community in the contemporary world (Putnam, 2001; Skocpol, 2004), it is important to be open to the possibility that powerful communities may emerge in unexpected spaces and sites over the next generation (a point also made by McKibben, 2008, 2011). Indeed, virtual 'communities' may turn out to be far more durable and influential spaces of community and political life in the future than anticipated. Certainly we can expect the growth trend in Internet use to continue given projections about the expanding reach of technology as a result of globalisation, a trend that will be further facilitated by rising transportation costs associated with peak oil (McKibben, 2011). All of these possible—and likely—futures foreshadow further growth in social networks and online communities, as well as greater expansion of the knowledge commons by ordinary citizens.

Furthermore, this Web 2.0 revolution carries the promise of making our social networks more transnational and more global. We can now connect easily with people across vast geographic distances. Social network theory suggests that because Web 2.0 technologies help increase the density of bonding relationships, people will be influenced to think about social situations in much broader and increasingly international terms.

In a related vein, another likely future associated with the reality of Web 2.0 information sharing is that processes of globalisation will be hastened. Digital space offers a new scaling of the global that is spatially distinct from cities and nations. As Sassen (2007, p. 234) notes: 'exploring these global digital spaces requires a specific conceptual architecture', one that is only beginning to be developed. As a result, she calls for a 'Sociology of Global Digital Spaces' to better understand the dynamic relationship between digital technologies, the global economy, and social life. Her work draws particular attention to the way that 'digitization increases mobility, including of what we have customarily thought of as immobile or barely mobile'. Here, Sassen is emphasising the way the Internet allows people and their ideas to travel virtually—a point we have made here as well—making the world much smaller for us all and creating new opportunities for political and social engagement with people in other nations. There is every reason to believe that the virtual mobility provided by the Internet will be increasingly important given the way that world is being newly re-bordered to constrain human mobility, particularly for the poor (Wonders, 2006, 2008).

There are, of course, risks associated with the digital knowledge commons. The dystopic side to this process of content sharing within social networks is the real tendency toward narrowing the scope of information made accessible within established communities (Sunstein, 2009) and the tendency toward anti-democratic, demagogic position taking. Also, it is important to consider that resource rich individuals, organisations, and agencies will be able to lower costs of access for themselves and use the technology to amplify their voice above the voices of others (Hendricks & Denton, 2010; Solop, 2010). It is also potentially easy to manufacture facts and information, and to encourage the distribution of 'trash' knowledge or engage in rumour-mongering. But, in many respects, that has always been true, regardless of the historic moment or the information medium.

Perhaps the best way to come to terms with the new knowledge commons is to adopt a 'stance of curiosity, rather than recognition, toward claims of truth' (Gibson-Graham, 2006, p. xxxi); in other words, it may be best to acknowledge 'the ultimate undecidability of meaning and the constitutive power of discourse, calling into question received ideas and dominant practices... and demonstrating how alternative forms of practice and power can emerge' (Gibson-Graham, 2006, p. 55). The socially constructed and tentative nature of knowledge is likely hard to embrace for 'digital immigrants'—those who have come to learn how to use digital technologies after being socialised into an analogue world. However, for 'digital natives', digital technology has always been present and has always shaped the way that they make meaning out of reality and the larger world (Palfrey & Gasser, 2008). For them, it is probably less problematic to embrace the notion that information and meaning are *created*. At the same time, we suspect that the current generation of Web 2.0 users will eventually desire new strategies for assessing the validity of truth claims; for this reason, a new form of reality hunger may well be on the horizon.

Concluding remarks

Just as David Shields' work reveals a literary form that allows for aggregated information and the repurposing of others' creative contributions, this article reveals how ordinary citizens are engaging in new kinds of information retrieval, production, and distribution. They too are hungry for reality—a reality they help to create. As we have analysed here, this new form of information construction is synergistically related to the development of Web 2.0 technology, which allows for easy access to huge swaths of information, extraction of information samples, information linking, and aggregating—and ultimately information production and redistribution by ordinary people.

By highlighting key features of the Web 2.0 information revolution, particularly the development of new forms of information production and diffusion through sampling and linking, we hope to deepen analytic thinking about knowledge production. Our goal is to encourage new research on public versus private control over information production and distribution, the power of social networks in the digital age, and the potential of Web 2.0 technologies for democracy and the creation of a new digital commons.

It is evident that the challenge for the future of information content is no longer how to digitise and distribute the information to wide audiences across a huge geographic area. Content aggregators already accomplish this task. The task now is how to best understand the importance and value of the information that is now being transmitted across social networks, to further explore the impact of these processes on political discourse and social life, and to adopt an attitude of 'reality hunger' toward the democratic potential of the new knowledge commons currently under construction.

Notes

1. Text and citations are formatted in the style of David Shields (2010): (1) Anna Tsing, *Friction*, 269; (2) Saskia Sassen, *A Sociology of Globalization*, 80–81; (3) Anna Tsing, *Friction*, 271; (4) David Shields, *Reality Hunger*, 40; (5) Saskia Sassen, *A Sociology of Globalization*, 81; (6) M. Lane Bruner, *Democracy's Debt* 293; (7) David Shields, *Reality Hunger*, 31; and (8) David Shields, *Reality Hunger*, 204, quoting John Berger, G: *A Novel* (this is the fragment Shields uses to conclude his manifesto).
2. Available online at: http://technorati.com/blogs/directory (accessed 1 March 2012).
3. National Public Radio (2011) 'Digital Music Sampling: Criminality or Creativity' (January 28). Available online at: http://www.npr.org/2011/01/28/133306353/Digital-Music-Sampling-Creativity-Or-Criminality (accessed 20 March 2011).
4. Available online at: http://www.geekosystem.com/hyperlink-book (accessed 22 March 2011).
5. While we highlight the potential of Web 2.0 activities to increase 'personal power' and social networking, it is important to note that sampling and linking occur within Web 2.0 applications dominated by private companies (like *Facebook*) which have other goals, including profit maximization. The tension between public and private benefits of Web 2.0 provides fertile ground for future social science research.
6. See https://www.Facebook.com/press/info.php?statistics#!/press/info.php?statistics (accessed March 2011).
7. See Facebook statistics as referenced in previous endnote and accessed 7 October 2011. Only China and India have larger populations than then number of active Facebook users.
8. See http://www.pamorama.net/2011/01/05/content-sharing-trends-in-2010-infographic/ (accessed 6 October 2011).
9. See http://static.businessinsider.com/~/f?id=4a66226414b9b98a00db2471 (accessed 6 October 2011).
10. Some books that might stimulate thinking along these lines include Watts (2004) and Barabasi (2002).

References

AllTechnoblog (2010) How social engagement is changing [INFOGRAPHIC]. Available online at: http://alltechnoblog.com/how-social-engagement-is-changing-infographic (accessed 11 August 2010).

Andarson, J. & Rainie, L. (2010) Millennials will make online sharing in networks a lifelong habit. Pew Charitable Trusts, July 9. Available online at: http://pewinternet.org/Reports/2010/Future-of-Millennials/Overview.aspx?r=1 (accessed 1 March 2012).

Bagdikian, B. (2004) *The new media monopoly* (Boston, MA, Beacon Press).

Barabasi, A. (2002) *Linked: the new science of networks* (Cambridge, MA, Perseus Publishing).
Bruner, M. L. (2009) *Democracy's debt: the historical tensions between political and economic liberty* (Amherst, NY, Humanity Books).
Cohen, P. (2010) Analyzing literature by words and numbers, *New York Times* (December 3). Available online at: http://www.nytimes.com/2010/12/04/books/04victorian.html (accessed 3 October 2011).
Boyd, D. M. & Ellison, N. B. (2007) Social network sites: definition, history, and scholarship, *Journal of Computer-Mediated Communication*, 13(1), article 11. Available online at: http://jcmc.indiana.edu/vol13/issue1/boyd.ellison.html.
Boyle, P. (2010) *The public domain: enclosing the commons of the mind* (New Haven, CT, Yale University Press).
de Zúñiga, H. G., Veenstra, A., Vraga, E. & Shah, D. (2010) Digital democracy: reimagining pathways to political participation, *Journal of Information Technology & Politics*, 7(1), 36–51.
Finen, T., Joshi, A., Kolari, P., Java, A., Kale, A. & Karandikar, A. (2008) The information ecology of social media and online communities, *Artificial Intelligence Magazine*, 29(3), 77–92.
Frey, J. (2005) *A million little pieces* (New York, Anchor Books).
Gibson-Graham, J. K. (2006) *A postcapitalist politics* (Minneapolis, MN, University of Minnesota Press).
Goodwin, A. (1988) Sample and hold: pop music in the age of digital reproduction, *Critical Quarterly*, 30(3), 34–49.
Hendricks, J. A. & Denton Jr, R. E. (Eds) (2010) *Communicator in Chief: how Barack Obama used new media technology to win the White House* (New York, Lexington Books).
Jensen, M. J., Danziger, J. N. & Venkatesh, A. (2007) Civil society and cyber society: the role of the Internet in community associations and democratic politics, *The Information Society*, 23, 39–50.
Lethem, J. (2007) The ecstasy of influence: a plagiarism, *Harpers* (February). Available online at: http://harpers.org/archive/2007/02/0081387 (accessed 23 March 2011).
Mackay, J. B. (2010) Gadgets, gismos, and the Web 2.0 election, in: J. A. Hendricks & R. E. Denton J (Eds) *Communicator-in-Chief: how Barack Obama used new media technology to win the White House* (New York, Lexington Books), 19–35.
McKibben, B. (2008) *Deep economy: the wealth of communities and the durable future* (New York, St. Martina's Griffin).
McKibben, B. (2011) *Eaarth: making a life on a tough new planet* (New York, St. Martina's Griffin).
Menzies, H. (2005) *No time: stress and the crisis of modern life* (Vancouver, Douglas & McIntyre).
Milgram, S. (1967) The small world problem, *Psychology Today*, (May), 60–67.
Morrison, B. (2010) Realty Hunger: a manifesto by David Shields, *The Guardian*, Available online at: http://www.guardian.co.uk/books/2010/feb/20/reality-hunger-david-shields-review (accessed 6 October 2011).
National Public Radio (2011) Digital music sampling: criminality or creativity (January 28). Available online at: http://www.npr.org/2011/01/28/133306353/Digital-Music-Sampling-Creativity-Or-Criminality (accessed 20 March 2011).
Palfrey, J. & Gasser, U. (2008) *Born digital: understanding the first generation of digital natives* (New York, Basic Books).
Parenti, M. (2010) *Democracy for the few* (Boston, MA, Wadsworth Publishing).
Pariser, E. (2011) *The filter bubble: what the Internet is hiding from you* (New York, Penguin Press).
Pew Research Center (2011) The State of the News Media 2011 (February). Available online at: http://stateofthemedia.org/2011/overview-2/key-findings (accessed 21 March 2011).
Ponte, L. M. (2006) The Emperor Has No Clothes: how digital sampling infringement cases are exposing weaknesses in traditional copyright law and the need for statutory reform, *American Business Law Journal*, 43(3), 515–560.
Putnam, R. (2001) *Bowling alone: the collapse and revival of American community* (New York, Touchstone Books).
Sassen, S. (2007) *A sociology of globalization* (New York, W.W. Norton & Company).
Schor, J. B. (2010) *Plentitude: the new economics of true wealth* (New York, Penguin).
Shields, D. (2010) *Reality Hunger: a manifesto* (New York, Knopf).
Schumate, M. & Dewitt, L. (2008) The north/south divide in NGO hyperlink networks, *Journal of Computer-Mediated Communication*, 13, 405–428.
Schumate, M. & Lipp, J. (2008) Connective collective action Online: an examination of the hyperlink network structure of an NGO issue network, *Journal of Computer-Mediated Communication*, 14, 178–201.
Skocpol, T. (2004) *Diminished democracy: from membership to management in American civic life* (Norman, OK, University of Oklahoma Press).
Solop, F. I. (2001) Digital democracy comes of age: Internet voting and the 2000 Arizona Democratic Primary Election, *Political Science & Politics*, 34, 289–293.
Solop, F. I. (2010) RT @BarackObama we just made history: Twitter and the 2008 Presidential Election, in: J. A. Hendricks & R. E. Denton Jr (Eds) *Communicator-in-Chief: a look at how Barack Obama used new media technology to win the White House* (Lanham, MD, Lexington Books), 37–49.
Sunstein, C. R. (2009) *Republic.com 2.0* (Princeton, NJ, Princeton University Press).
Tsing, A. (2004) *Friction: an ethnography of global connection* (Princeton, NJ, Princeton University Press).

Vergeer, M. & Hermans, L. (2008) Analysing online political discussions: methodological considerations, *Javnost–The Public*, 15(2), 37–56.

Waldman, S. (2011) The information needs of communities: the changing media landscape in a broadband age (July). Washington, DC: Federal Communications Commission. Available online at: http://transition.fcc.gov/osp/inc-report/The_Information_Needs_of_Communities.pdf (accessed 5 October 2011).

Watts, D. (2003) *Six degrees: the science of a connected age* (New York, W. W. Norton & Company).

Weber, M. S. & Monge, P. (2011) The flow of digital news in a network of authorities, sources and hubs, *Journal of Communication*, 61, 1062–1081.

Wonders, N. (2006) Global flows, semi-permeable borders and new channels of inequality: border crossers and border performativity, in: S. Pickering & L. Weber (Eds) *Borders, mobility and technologies of control* (Dordrecht, The Netherlands, Springer Publishing), 62–86.

Wonders, N. (2008) Globalization, border reconstruction projects, and transnational crime, *Social Justice*, 34(2), 33–46.

An illustrated framework for the analysis of Web2.0 interactivity

Peter Mechant
MICT/IBBT/UGent, Ghent, Belgium

The importance and significance of participation and engagement through interactivity on Web2.0 sites emerge in the literature about Web2.0. In order to gain insight into interactivity on Web2.0 platforms, and thus to assess the impact of Web2.0, we develop an analytical framework. Based on a conceptual analysis of interaction, a phrase omnipresent in the discourse on new communication technologies, the internet and Web2.0 in particular, our framework takes into account the objective, structural features of Web2.0 platforms (expressed in structural affordances) and the functional, subjective perception and usage of these features by the users of these Web2.0 platforms (expressed in functional affordances). In order to test the value and usefulness of this analytical framework, we set up a small, qualitative research design ($N = 27$). Our goal was to use the developed framework to explore how agency and engagement on Flickr and deviantART, two Web2.0 sites, are reflected in the use of Web2.0 affordances and thus demonstrate the usability and value of the developed framework. We conclude that the analytical framework enables us to describe the interactivity that plays out on Flickr and deviantART as websites 'through' which internet users can communicate, as well as sites 'with' which internet users can communicate. Flickr and deviantART are spaces where interaction 'goes beyond' the mere consultation and selection of content, as they support the (co)creation of content and processes of collective or individual agency. The developed analytical framework thus provides insight into the emancipatory or participatory potential of these websites, showing that our respondents consider Flickr and deviantART to be meeting places for photo- or art-lovers and suggesting that the websites function as virtual 'third places'.

Introduction

It is widely recognized that Western internet users have increasingly appropriated Web2.0 websites. Web2.0, understood as a large-scale shift towards a participatory and collaborative version of the web, enables internet users to 'get involved' and create or share content (Beer, 2009), thus supporting and mutually maximizing collective intelligence and added value for each participant (Hoegg et al., 2006).

On Web2.0 platforms, content is created not internally at the internet companies (Jakobsson & Stiernstedt, 2010) but by the users themselves (Hudson-Smith *et al.*, 2009).

Several authors such as O'Reilly (2003), Jaokar (2006) and Hoegg *et al.* (2006) emphasize the goal of Web2.0 websites and services. They state that 'creating network effects through an architecture of participation' is the central principle of Web2.0 and that all other Web2.0 principles feed into this idea. Others explore the ideological meanings and the social, political and ethical implications of Web2.0. Scholz (2008), for example, argues that Web2.0 functions as a framing device. Other authors explore the role of Web2.0 as a tool or a framework for (peer) surveillance (Albrechtslund, 2008; Zimmer, 2008) or critique Web2.0 as the increased corporatization of online social and collaborative spaces and content (Jarrett, 2008; Petersen, 2008). From this viewpoint, Web2.0 does not provide an 'architecture of participation' (O'Reilly, 2003) but rather provides an 'architecture of exploitation that capitalism can benefit from' (Petersen, 2008).

Although Web2.0 has become one of the central concepts in contemporary discussions about the internet, the actual meaning of Web2.0 is still subject to discussion with various authors emphasizing the hyped character of the phrase (Stern & Wakabayashi, 2007). Moreover, although the importance and significance of participation and engagement through interactivity on Web2.0 sites emerge in the literature, a contextual framework for the analysis of interactivity on Web2.0 sites in objective, structural terms as well as in subjective, functional terms is missing.

The purpose of this article is to address this shortcoming by developing an analytical framework based on a conceptual analysis of interactivity. In the first section of the article, the concept 'interactivity' is theoretically unpacked and approached as a multidimensional concept encompassing user-to-user, user-to-document and user-to-website interactivity. Next, an analytical framework, which takes into account structure and agency, is proposed. This framework for Web2.0 interactivity provides researchers with a descriptive vocabulary and a methodological approach for exploring the meaning and significance of Web2.0 sites for internet users. In the third section, the value and usefulness of this analytical framework are tested using a qualitative, small-scale and exploratory research design targeted at Flickr and deviantART users. Next, results are described and discussed, focusing on how participation on Flickr and deviantART is reflected in the use of their affordances. The article ends with a conclusion on the value of the proposed multidimensional interactivity-based approach for the study of agency and engagement of internet users and links this to the exploratory study of interactivity on Flickr and deviantART.

Interactivity unpacked

In most general terms, the phrase 'interactivity' describes an active relationship between two things. Interactivity refers to an activity that involves interaction but is also used to point to the property of being interactive. The phrase 'interactivity' is rarely specified or defined (Rafaeli, 1988; McMillan & Downes, 2000). Jensen

(1999) notes that there is no consensus on the characteristics or dimensions of interactivity within the scientific community.

Interactivity is a concept that is often mentioned in relation to new media and the (theoretical) discourse on new communication technologies. Since the mid-1980s, communication scholars, particularly in the discipline of computer-mediated communication, have been working on the concept of interactivity (McMillan, 2002), and early in the study of the internet and the www, scientists identified interactivity as one of the main features of the web. Hence, interactivity grew, especially in the early years of the new millennium, into a real 'buzz' word. It became a concept that is often inappropriately used as a label or a selling point for new (communication) technologies (Quiring, 2009).

We distinguish three perspectives on interactivity in the literature (Kiousis, 2002; Leiner & Quiring, 2008; Tremayne, 2008; Quiring, 2009). These perspectives can be summarized as 'structure', 'process' and 'users' (McMillan & Downes, 2000). The first perspective ('structure') positions interactivity as a feature of a media technology, as 'a measure of a media's potential ability to let the user exert an influence on the content and/or form of the mediated communication' (Jensen & Toscan, 1999, p. 59). The second perspective ('process') describes interactivity as a communication process. The focus here is not on the analysis of technological characteristics but on the study of interactivity as a form of information exchange between different parties. From this 'process' viewpoint, interactivity is a 'cyclical process in which two actors alternately listen, think and speak' (Crawford, 2002, p. 6). The third perspective ('users') approaches interactivity as 'an information-based process that takes place within the individual' (Newhagen, 2004, p. 397). This viewpoint studies the effect of interactive communication channels and emphasizes the perception of the user. Interactivity thus becomes a 'function of both the inclusion of interactive tools as well as of the language used when offering that tool' (Lilleker & Malagon, 2010, p. 27).

In general, three traditions of interactivity research are identified: human-to-human, human-to-documents and human-to-system interactions, focusing, respectively, on human communication, on how people interact with content and on how people interact with the computer (or any type of new media system) (McMillan, 2002). From within these traditions, interactivity refers to the features of a medium (its potential for interaction in general) and to the extent that people will use these features or affordances. An important approach to interactivity focuses on the information streams between the sender and the receiver. From this perspective, it distinguishes three interactivity types: user-to-user, user-to-document and user-to-website interactivity (Szuprowicz, 1995; McMillan, 2002).

A framework for Web2.0 interactivity

Structural affordances

Using this distinction between user-to-user, user-to-document and user-to-website interactivity, we create Figure 1 that describes the Web2.0 features that afford such interactions. We call these features the structural affordances of a Web2.0 site. Thus, the interactive potential of a Web2.0 site is expressed in the site's structural affordances and in user, document and website affordances.

Roughly speaking, an affordance is what one system provides to another system, in our case what Web2.0 systems provide to their users. An affordance also encompasses the perceived functional significance of a website feature for an individual. Affordances have a complex if active history in ecological psychology and other disciplines (Hogan, 2009). For our purposes, we use the definition given by Norman (2002) describing affordances as 'the perceived and actual properties of the thing, primarily those fundamental properties that determine just how the thing could possibly be used' (p. 9).

User affordances encompass website features targeted at other internet users, enabling communication (e.g. a 'shoutbox' or an instant messaging tool), collaboration (e.g. a mutual event calendar) or networking (e.g. adding a 'friend' or joining a group). Document affordances refer to features that enable Web2.0 users to interact with content: for example, functions for search (e.g. a search box or a list with the most popular artists), features for content creation (e.g. assigning tags or writing comments) and features for user control (e.g. determining who is allowed to look at one's recent activities). Website affordances provide features for interaction between users and the websites, such as profile creation (e.g. adding a profile picture to the website), uploading content, adaptive interactivity (e.g. content customization or changing the look and feel of the website) and social awareness (e.g. consulting the recent activity of a user).

Affordances are a supremely relational concept because they link the external environment and internal states of mind. As affordances are the things that we recognize rather than the networks or website structure that we infer, they offer a key and

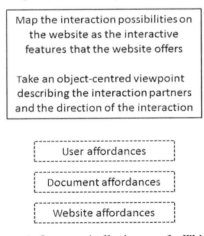

Figure 1. Structural affordances of a Web2.0 site

under-recognized link in a theory of structure and agency (Hogan, 2009). Web2.0 sites assemble a cohesive set of structural affordances that correspond closely to the website's goal and users. Thus, insight into the structural affordances of a Web2.0 platform provides knowledge about the performative infrastructure that the website supplies to internet users.

Functional affordances

As Web2.0 sites offer integrated affordances and boundaries around which Web2.0 users participate, insight into how these structural affordances are used is essential in order to analyse how agency and engagement of Web2.0 users are expressed. Thus, we also need a framework that describes how internet users engage and interact with the structural affordances mentioned above. Hence, we suggest to add a set of functional affordances (see Figure 2), namely inter-action, intra-action and outer-action affordances.

Inter-action affordances refer to the use of structural affordances for communication. Inter-action affordances, as the means for a communication process, reflect the use of structural affordances from a 'process' viewpoint: as a form of information exchange between two or more internet users. They enable conversations (see also 'conversational affordances', Reid & Reid, 2010) and can be described as 'social' affordances. We use the work of Hwang *et al.* (2009, p. 225) to define intra-action affordances as affordances enabling interaction

> from a person to himself/herself and time separation is essential (as space separation is not applicable). As the individual receiving the message is (due to time separation) in a different state from the moment when the message was issued, the message is likely to

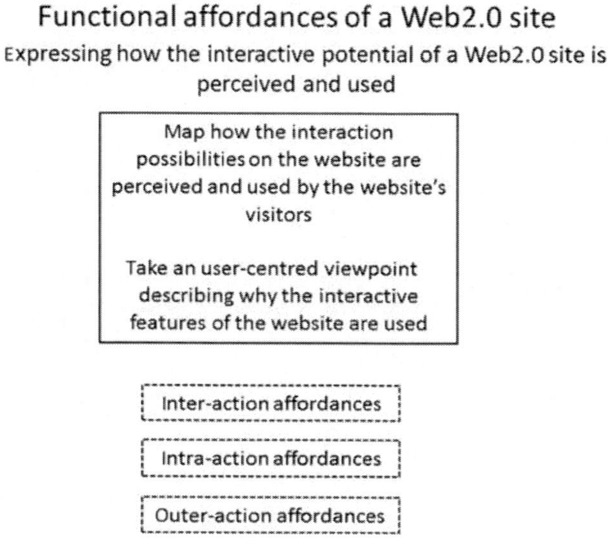

Functional affordances of a Web2.0 site
Expressing how the interactive potential of a Web2.0 site is perceived and used

Map how the interaction possibilities on the website are perceived and used by the website's visitors

Take an user-centred viewpoint describing why the interactive features of the website are used

Inter-action affordances

Intra-action affordances

Outer-action affordances

Figure 2. Functional affordances of a Web2.0 site

contain something 'new' and hence, valuable to the receiver, something that is not in his/her immediate field of attention, and yet, pertinent to his/her overall goals.

Intra-action does not refer to a mental or cognitive process but describes the process of external representation of the mental process. Hence, intra-action affordances can also be called 'personal' affordances. Building on the work of Nardi *et al.* (2000), we describe outer-action affordances as affordances supporting 'a set of communicative processes *outside of* information exchange, in which people *reach out* to others in patently social ways to enable information exchange' (p. 79). Thus, outer-action affordances enable negotiations about availability, enable finding ways to establish connection and enable the work of managing the progress of an interaction. We describe outer-action affordances as 'context' affordances. Outer-action affordances scaffold information exchange and play an important role in awareness systems intended to help people construct and maintain awareness of each other's activities, context or status.

Functional inter-action, intra-action and outer-action affordances are rarely used independently. For example, structural affordances may be first used as outer-action affordances communicating a simple greeting in the Web2.0 environment or indicating a person's availability. Next, once rapport is established, structural affordances may be used as inter-action affordances supporting communication between the website users. After the conversation, an internet user might use a structural affordance as an intra-action affordance, for example, by tagging or storing parts of the conversation as a message to oneself at a later moment in time.

Structural and functional affordances as a twofold framework

Combining the structural and functional affordance typologies results in a twofold analytical lens or framework enabling us to describe interactivity on Web2.0 sites in objective, structural terms as well as in subjective, functional terms. Structural affordances show us Web2.0 as a space of object-oriented user, document and website affordances. Functional affordances describe Web2.0 as a space of perceived inter-action (social), intra-action (personal) and outer-action (context) affordances. This twofold framework for Web2.0 interactivity thus takes into account structure and agency, synthesizing both the structural properties of the Web2.0 environment and the ways that users perceive and interact with these capabilities.

Web2.0 users will often resort to user affordances (as social affordances) to set up conversations with others, they will use document affordances (as personal affordances) to interact with the Web2.0 content and they will often use website affordances (as context affordances) to communicate and interact with the Web2.0 platform itself. This shows that there are strong parallels between both components of the twofold analytical framework. Juxtaposition of structural and functional affordances shows that (1) structural user affordances can be linked to functional inter-action or 'social' affordances; (2) structural document affordances can be linked to functional intra-action or 'personal' affordances and (3) structural website affordances can be linked to functional outer-action or 'context' affordances. Figure 3 summarizes the components of the twofold framework for the analysis of interactivity in Web2.0 environments.

Although we hypothesize strong parallels between the structural and functional components of our analytical framework, their relation differs sometimes. Such deviations or differences are of utmost importance and emphasize the true meaning or significance of the Web2.0 site for the user(s), reflecting his or her commitment and engagement on that site. Literature on 'tagging' (assigning labels to content), for example, shows that 'tagging' as a structural document affordance is used as a functional intra-action and outer-action affordance (Golder & Huberman, 2005, 2006; Hammond et al., 2005). In other words, some users tag as part of an externalization of a personal and cognitive process, assigning organizational or selfish tags for their personal benefit or goal (tagging used as an intra-action affordance), while others assign social or altruistic tags for yet others to retrieve and use (tagging used as an outer-action affordance).

Applying the framework to the websites Flickr and deviantART

Flickr and deviantART

In order to test the value and usefulness of the analytical framework, we set up a small, qualitative research design. Our goal was to use the developed framework to explore how agency and engagement on Web2.0 sites are reflected in the use of Web2.0 affordances and thus demonstrate the usability and value of the developed framework. We decided to apply this research question to two Web2.0 sites: Flickr.com and deviantART.com. Our research question was formulated as follows: 'How are the agency and engagement of Flickr users and deviantART users reflected in the use of the websites' affordances?'.

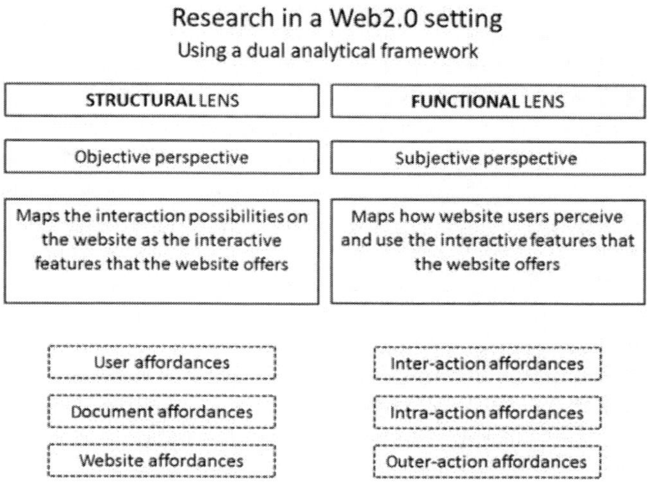

Figure 3. Components of the twofold framework

The first website, Flickr, is often mentioned in the literature as an archetypical Web2.0 site (e.g. Miller, 2005; O'Reilly, 2005; Alexander, 2006; Maness, 2006; Cox, 2007; Pissard & Prieur, 2007; Prieur *et al.*, 2008; Breslin *et al.*, 2009; Valafar *et al.*, 2009) and was launched during the Web2.0 hype in February 2004 by the couple Stewart Butterfield and Caterina Fake out of one of the components of the online multiplayer game 'Game Neverending' (Prieur *et al.*, 2008). The website enables internet users to access a huge repository of photographs and to a lesser extent (short) video clips. Registered users can upload photographs and video clips on Flickr and can share them with others. They also have affordances at their disposal to edit, enrich and organize their content and to network and communicate with other Flickr users. Each registered Flickr user, also known as 'Flickrite', has a profile page and a page displaying the user's 'photostream'. Registering on Flickr is free. However, users who pay a small fee have access to premium services not available for non-paying users. The *British Journal of Photography* reported in early 2009 that Flickr had 47 million members (Laurent, 2009). On Flickr's help fora, a figure of similar magnitude is mentioned. However, Valafar *et al.* (2009), based on extrapolation network analysis, reported a figure of 25 million users. Flickr is among the top 50 most visited websites in the world according to the Alexa WebMonitor and is visited monthly by about 45 million internet users according to Google's Adplanner. For Flanders (the northern part of Belgium), the region where the respondents were recruited, figures from DigiMeter, an annual survey on the adoption and use of ICT, show that about 5% of the Flemish internet users have a user account on Flickr (De Marez & Schuurman, 2010, 2011).

The second site, deviantART, is less frequently associated with Web2.0 (e.g. Christodoulou & Styliaras, 2008; Rigby, 2008; Conole & Alevizou, 2010), probably because its launch was situated well before the phrase 'Web2.0' attracted lots of buzz and attention. deviantART.com was launched in the middle of the dot.com burst (August 2000) by Scott Jarkoff, Angelo Sotira and Matt Stephens as part of a larger network of music-related websites called the Dmusic Network. Although initially focused on displaying skins (custom graphical appearances for software), the website took the concept further and moved towards an art community that was very lenient for 'deviant' artworks, ensuring their members freedom of expression with as few restrictions as possible. deviantART wants to enable emerging and established artists to exhibit, promote and share their works within a peer community dedicated to the arts. Thus, deviantART users, also known as 'deviants', have profile pages and exhibition spaces (galleries). They can converse about art in one of the online discussion fora or in the chatrooms of deviantART. They have social networking features at their disposal and can comment on and interact with the artwork on deviantART (also known as deviations). deviantART is strongly status-focused: by means of different punctuation marks in front of user names, the status of deviants is expressed (e.g. ~ = member, * = premium member, ' = senior member). Moreover, analogous to Flickr, internet users who pay a small amount have access to premium accounts offering features not available or restricted for non-paying deviants. According to QuantCast.com, deviantART is visited monthly by 26.7 million internet users. On deviantART, accounts cannot be deleted, making it difficult to assess the total number of active registered deviantART users (about 25% of deviantART accounts are presumed to be 'inactive', Rosadiuk, 2008). Figures revealed by deviantART's CEO Sotira in his closing speech on the occasion of deviantART's 10th birthday show that deviantART counted 14.4 million registered users who submit 140,000 deviations, add 1.4 million deviations to their favourites, place 1.5 million comments and send 220,000 notes on a daily basis (Sotira, 2010). For Flanders, no membership figures exist. However, based on observations of the website and on earlier research on internet use in Flanders, we suggest that the percentage of all the Flemish internet users participating on deviantART is significantly lower than that participating on Flickr.

Recruitment

We chose a 'purposeful' sampling strategy and recruitment method (Strauss & Corbin, 1998; Patton, 2002), selecting information-rich research topics for in-depth analysis and study. Purposeful sampling is a form of judgement sampling where the researcher 'actively selects the most productive sample to answer the research question' (Marshall, 1996, p. 523). We tried to recruit respondents who comply with a specific segmentation of Flemish media users, described as 'new media freaks' by DigiMeter (De Marez & Schuurman, 2010, 2011). These media users make up about 20% of the Flemish population and show the highest usage of computer, internet and Web2.0 sites. They also have the highest self-estimation in terms of digital skills and are the most active in adding online content. In order to select these respondents, we used various criteria based on the description of the 'new media freaks' segment (De Marez & Schuurman, 2010, 2011) as well as on group discussions and consultation meetings with university students and colleagues, and a literature review of and (participative) observation on the websites Flickr and deviantART.

During the recruitment phase, we targeted a 'maximum variety sample' (Morse, 1998), ensuring that the sample was heterogeneous with core observable commonalities of experience (Patmore *et al.*, 2001). In order for a Flemish Flickrite to be recruited, he or she had to comply with at least two of the following criteria: the number of photos uploaded had to be greater than 100; the number of memberships to groups had to be greater than 50; the number of favourites added to the profile had to be greater than 200 and/or the person had to be a 'pro' Flickr user (has a paid, premium account). In order for a Flemish deviant to be recruited, he or she had to comply with at least three of the following criteria: the number of deviations watched was greater than 1000; the number of deviations uploaded was greater than 50; the number of comments placed was greater than 100; the number of favourites added was greater than 500 and/or the deviant account was created prior to February 2009 (deviantART member for at least a year).

It is important to note that, like any qualitative sample, ours does not claim to be representative for Flemish users of Flickr or deviantART. However, we are convinced that the sample consists of internet users who frequently engage with new media and

Web2.0 sites. In that sense, all respondents can be categorized as 'new media freaks' or frequent Web2.0 users. This has some important methodological and theoretical implications. For one thing: the value of the developed framework can only be assessed for the study of this type of internet users. Also, results and conclusions on the agency and engagement on Flickr and deviantART need to be interpreted in this context and cannot be generalized to those who use the same technology (far) less frequently.

Sample description

In total, 27 respondents were recruited (12 deviants and 15 Flickrites) with an average age of 27.4 years. Sixty per cent of the sample was male ($N = 16$). The majority of the respondents ($N = 18$) spent more than 2 h online on an average day. Only a small fraction of the sample ($N = 3$) spent less than an hour online on a daily basis.

The recruited Flickrites were very Web2.0-savy, with all of them having a Facebook account and with more than two-thirds having accounts on instant messaging applications and social bookmarking websites. Also, more than half of the respondents ($N = 8$) managed a weblog. The same goes for the recruited deviants: except one, they all had a Facebook account. Also, the majority had an account on YouTube. Similar to the Flickr respondents, 8 of the 12 deviantART users had a weblog.

Tables 1 and 2 show how the deviantART respondents posted, on average, 177 deviations. For Flickr, this number is much higher: the Flickrites who were interviewed posted, on average, 3565 pictures. Further descriptive information is provided in Tables 1 and 2.

Questions and coding methodology

Between February and March 2010, we interviewed the 27 respondents separately using a semi-structured topic list (Fontana, 2002; Fontana & Frey, 2005). An interview took an average of 80 min. The interviews took place, as far as possible, in the vicinity of a computer so that the respondent could log into his or her account and illustrate his or her statements, habits and practices.

The semi-structured topic list served as a 'guide' during the conversations with the respondents and consisted questions on (1) the usage of the website and the meaning that the respondents assign to the website; (2) interactivity with other website users and the social aspect of using the website; (3) interactivity with the (user-generated) content on the website and (4) interactivity with the website itself.

In order to apply the twofold analytical framework that we developed, we used a deductive methodology to code the transcripts of the interviews. A deductive methodology enables coding through a predefined (theoretical) perspective (Berg, 2001). Deductive coding encompasses three coding phases (Miles & Huberman, 1994). In the first phase, descriptive codes are assigned to text snippets based on predefined areas of interest, whether factual, thematic or theoretical in nature (Lewins & Silver, 2007). We used the structural component of the twofold analytical framework

Table 1. Flickr respondents

Flickr respondents	Account type	Number of contacts	Number of favourites	Number of posted pictures	Membership (years)	Gender	Age
Jenny	Pro	133	72	939	2	F	39
John	Pro	157	582	4758	3	M	34
Miriam	Pro	83	136	1830	5	F	21
Isolde	Free	30	40	200	4	F	30
Tony	Pro	101	486	6450	5	M	30
Mike	Pro	253	265	4724	5	M	26
Pieter	Pro	6	49	2263	4	M	30
Marcel	Pro	12	2	524	3	M	44
Griet	Free	214	2556	161	2	F	22
Greta	Pro	69	2465	27,089	5	F	65
Steve	Free	20	20	151	2	M	22
Natalie	Pro	316	1489	117	4	F	22
Willem	Pro	65	45	1484	2	M	49
Bart	Pro	85	142	329	2	M	22
Ilse	Pro	180	132	2465	5	F	40
Mean		114	565	3565	3.5		33
Median		85	136	1484	4		30
St. Dev.		92	876	6802	1.3		12

encompassing three interaction classes (user, document and website interaction affordances) to assign codes describing the usage of the website features, thus gaining insight into *which* website features were used. Next, interpretative coding took place, digging deeper into the meaning of the descriptive codes. Here, we used the functional component of the twofold analytical framework encompassing three interaction classes (inter-action, intra-action and outer-action affordances) in order to describe *how* and *why* website features were used. Finally, moving on to a more inferential and explanatory level by examining the parallels, differences and oppositions between the descriptive and interpretative codes, we assigned pattern codes.

In this way, codes describing which website features were used were juxtapositioned to codes describing how and why these features were used. Using the structural component of the twofold analytical framework to assign descriptive codes and using the functional component of the twofold analytical framework to assign interpretative codes enabled us to compare, during the process of assigning pattern codes, the (technological) structure of the website with how the website is actually perceived and used. This cyclic coding process was iterated several times until no further insights could be extracted from the texts.

Results and discussion

Our research question targets agency and engagement on Flickr and deviantART and addresses how participation on a Web2.0 platform is reflected in the use of the

Table 2. deviantART respondents

deviantART respondents	Account type	Number of accounts watched/ being watched	Number of favourites	Number of posted deviations	Membership (years)	Gender	Age
Matthias	Senior	398/1266	1680	100	4	M	26
Britt	Premium	233/92	643	147	6	F	22
Els	Member	0/110	91	36	3	F	21
Roos	Beta tester	430/234	389	103	4	F	24
Chris	Premium	345/170	4141	180	6	M	30
Anja	Beta tester	–	777	398	7	F	24
Niels	Member	66/220	2316	27	3	M	20
Floor	Member	188/133	877	316	5	F	23
Ingrid	Member	57/53	44	49	6	F	22
Rudy	Senior	96/2101	204	67	4	M	25
David	Gallery moderator	1047/6620	684	178	6	M	26
Mark	Member	79/86	1893	525	3	M	37
Mean		267/1007	1144	177	4.7		25
Median		188/170	730	125	4.5		24
St. Dev.		297/1971	1192	157	1.4		5.4

websites' affordances. We structure our results in three sections. First, we describe how the structural user affordances of Flickr and deviantART are used. Next, we focus on document affordances on both websites, specifically on website features enabling tagging, faving and commenting. Finally, the usage of the website affordances of Flickr and deviantART is addressed. In each section, we also analyse these practices in terms of inter-action, intra-action and outer-action, thus reflecting on their functional significance.

User affordances

We defined affordances targeted at other internet users as structural user affordances. From a functional perspective, these are closely linked to inter-action or social affordances. Although our data show that, in general, user affordances are seldom activated by our respondents, we did find various examples of how users manage these affordances to converse, interact and network with others.

In contrast to the Flickr interviewees indicating that they do not send private messages (FlickrMail) or use the website extensively for networking, most Flickr respondents did mention that they actively seek membership of Flickr groups. Joining a group, however, not only functions as an inter-action or a social affordance but also has a very important role in creating an audience or a public for one's photographs, which illustrates how the affordance to join a group is used as an outer-action or a context affordance scaffolding future interactions:

> The first group I joined was the group 'ScoreMe', because members give points to each other's pictures. Now, I take pictures and then I start looking for groups where I can post my pictures. Especially in order to get comments on them. (Bart, Flickr pro, 22 years)

Except for the user affordance to create or join groups, most user affordances (enabling, for example, sending a private message or adding a contact to one's Flickr network) were not key for the Flickrites whom we interviewed. Isolde's quote is typical for their position:

> I like Flickr for the photos, and my photos especially, but the whole system of Flickr is not really for communication or interaction. The focus is only on those photos. Given that there is such a thing as Facebook, why do something else, why should I look for something else? (Flickr free, 30 years)

deviantART offers, in contrast to Flickr, a broad range of user affordances, enabling both synchronous and asynchronous interpersonal and group communication, as well as networking with other deviants and the surveillance of the work of others (through the deviantWATCH affordance). We noticed that these user affordances often serve as inter-action affordances enabling deviants to discuss a wide variety of topics in a wide variety of groups:

> I talk about anything and everything. That can really vary. It might be about politics, for example when there are elections... but also about stupid things in groups such as 'LOLcats'. So... it can sometimes be very serious but also very brain-less. (Niels, deviantART member, 20 years)

Document affordances

Structural document affordances are interaction features targeted at Web2.0 content elements. These document affordances are closely linked to intra-action or personal affordances from a functional perspective, reflecting the externalization of a cognitive process. We will discuss tagging, faving and commenting as the use of three main document affordances, enabling interactivity with Web2.0 content.

Our interviews show that on Flickr, the document affordance 'tagging' is mainly used as an 'intra-action' affordance, as a means to communicate to oneself or organize photographs for oneself. In addition, 'tagging' also serves as an outer-action affordance, because assigning sufficient and clear labels to one's photographs helps making them visible and searchable. Likewise, on deviantART, 'tagging' content is most often an 'intra-action'. Moreover, as outer-action, the inappropriate use of tags is despised by all deviants we talked to:

> Yes, I tag my deviations, but I do not misuse the system. I assign 'to-the-point' tags such as 'make up', 'wig', 'medieval' or 'fantasy' and such. But I do not misuse tags. That is very annoying; some people tag their deviations with tags such as 'sex', 'porn' or 'girls'. Others use very generic words, thus polluting the search system. I hate those kind of deviants! (Britt, deviantART premium, 22 years)

With regard to 'faving' (adding a content element to his or her list of favourites), we noticed two functional dimensions. Most Flickr and deviantART respondents indicated that they primarily use this document affordance type to add a photograph or an artwork to his or her private collection of interesting and beautiful photographs or artworks, thus creating an own art or photography collection (using the document affordance as an intra-action affordance). Other Flickrites or deviants told us that they add content to their favourites because, in this way, they can communicate their appreciation to the photographer or artist (using the document affordance as an inter-action affordance). The following quote shows that the 'faving' affordance can be used alternately as a social or an inter-action affordance or as a personal or an intra-action affordance:

> Sometimes I assign photos of others to my favourites. Sometimes, I do this to show the creator that I find his or her work really good, without having to put much effort in it. Most often however, I just try to create a collection of beautiful things. (Jenny, Flickr pro, 39 years)

Our respondents use commenting, the last document affordance that we discuss, sparingly. Often they refer to the phatic or trivial character of most comments to explain why they do not use this structural document affordance. Still, sometimes comments are used to gather and give constructive, positive feedback on others' work and to start conversations. We note that the respondents use this document affordance as a social affordance: they seek a conversation or a dialogue about the photograph or artwork:

> When I want to give a comment, it is never a comment like 'nice picture' or 'well done'. I find such comments pointless and try to offer real feedback. I write, for example, 'That's a pretty composition with that pole on the right ..., well done, I would do it a bit more so and so'. There are so many 'empty' comments written on the internet that it gets on my nerves sometimes. (Tony, Flickr pro, 30 years)

In this respect, we would like to point to the special document affordance 'Critique'. This affordance was implemented in April 2009 on deviantART and is only available to premium deviantART members. 'Critique' was created to avoid the phatic or meaningless content that was submitted through the 'normal' comment affordance of deviantART. The 'Critique' feature was introduced to enable substantive criticism and feedback on deviations. deviantART emphasizes the profound, thoughtful and respectful character of a 'Critique' describing it in its Frequently Asked Questions section as 'designed to help artists get in-depth, critical feedback and commentary on their work. (...) The Critique system co-exists with the original comments system but provides a space that is designed for considered, thoughtful and RESPECTFUL criticism'.

Website affordances

Affordances that target interactivity with the Web2.0 website itself were defined, from a structural perspective, as website affordances. These affordances are, from a functional perspective, closely linked to outer-action or context affordances, enabling users to create a social framework and conditions that can support them in their future actions on the website.

Of course, on both Flickr and deviantART, the website affordance to upload content is of utmost importance for our respondents. This affordance enables them to share their content and strive for 'publicity'. Moreover, the website affordance of deviantART to upload content is appreciated and used because of its flexible, open and lenient character:

> I attend drawing classes and I now regularly draw nudes. The advantage [of deviantART] is that I can upload those drawings and sketches without being blocked. Other websites, for example, a social networking such as Netlog, block such content. When you are repeatedly blocked, they even deny you access. (Mark, deviantART member, 37 years)

Our respondents also presume the willingness to share and do not appreciate people who use the upload affordance as a means to create a personal, private archive of content, shared with no one:

> It is really a shame to use Flickr as a mere photo bucket, as a mere online repository. I use Flickr to share my photos and learn or pickup ideas from others. If nobody would share his or her photographs that would not be possible. (Natalie, Flickr free, 22 years)

Especially interesting are website affordances that communicate information from the website to the website user. Two of those website affordances are 'social navigation' and 'social browsing'. 'Social browsing' refers to content exploration based on the practices, uploads and preferences of one's social network on the website. 'Social navigation' refers to content exploration based on the practices, uploads and preferences of the whole website community. Our interviews show that both affordances, enabling adaptive interactivity between website and website user, are frequently used.

'Social browsing' was spontaneously mentioned by most respondents as an important way of finding new and interesting content on Flickr or deviantART:

> What I really like is to see my contacts' new photos. I take pictures with a Lomo ... in the Lomo group, of which I am member, every day new photographs appear and that's just interesting. (Isolde, Flickr free, 30 years)

'Social navigation' is also supported by website affordances. An example on Flickr includes the 'Interestingness' page that shows the 500 most interesting pictures of that day based on an algorithm that takes into account where the clickthroughs on a photo are coming from; who comments on the photo and when; who marks the photo as a favourite; its tags and many more things which are constantly changing.

Another website affordance supporting Flickrites in their practice of taking photographs is the automatic display of the Exif (exchangeable image file format) data of photos which helps them to gain insight into the technical aspects of a particular photograph. On deviantART, we encountered website affordances supporting adaptive interactivity such as the possibility of tweaking content presentation to show only content that fits the interests of the deviant. Other website affordances of deviantART support social awareness, displaying, for example, a community mood (the aggregation of individual moods of the deviants). Again, website affordances function as outer-action affordances, creating awareness of the communication environment and helping deviants to understand the website's context, thus supporting (future) inter-action and intra-action.

Conclusion

We conclude that the twofold analytical framework, developed in this article, enables us to describe the interactivity that plays out on Flickr and deviantART. Specifically, the framework provides insight into the agency and engagement of 'new media freaks'. The framework allows us to describe both websites in objective, structural terms as spaces of user, document and website affordances. The framework also makes it possible to talk about the two websites in subjective, functional terms, describing them as spaces of perceived inter-action, intra-action and outer-action affordances. The framework thus has three important merits.

First, it enables us to interpret Web2.0 as a medium 'through' which internet users can communicate as well as a medium 'with' which internet users can communicate. This perspective breaks with the instrumental view that considers, both in name and in function, the internet as an instrument or a medium. Nowadays, Web2.0 websites actively participate in communicative exchanges as a kind of additional agent and/or (inter)active co-conspirator in the interaction between Web2.0 users. Web2.0 platforms take the position of a social actor with whom one communicates and interacts, challenging longstanding assumptions about the role and function of technology.

Second, the elaborated framework allows for the analysis of Web2.0 sites as spaces where interaction 'goes beyond' the mere consultation and selection of content, as spaces supporting the (co)creation of content and value. In this respect, the framework can describe new communication patterns that extend on the four 'ideal information patterns' formulated by Bordewijk and van Kaam (1986) (see also Hoem, 2006).

Third, the framework takes into account structure and agency and helps us to understand processes of collective or individual agency, thus enabling further insight into the emancipatory or participatory potential of these spaces. This emancipatory power of the internet and its potential to revitalize democracy are being increasingly critically approached after a period of celebratory chronicles about the internet and the web (Curran et al., 2012).

Moreover, describing interactivity on Web2.0 sites in terms of affordances enables us to focus on the relationships between users and Web2.0 sites because the concept 'affordance' makes a connection between (the properties of) the environment (Web2.0 sites) and the cognitive and mental processes among the users of these sites. With our twofold framework, we integrate both the structural properties of Web2.0 (structure) and the ways that users interact with these capabilities (agency). The twofold framework thus takes into account human agency as well as the technological tools and components of the Web2.0 environment.

We can also conclude that the majority of our respondents consider Flickr and deviantART to be a meeting place for photo- or art-lovers, suggesting that the sites are virtual 'third places'. Virtual 'third places' are places that exists outside the home and beyond the 'work lots' of modern economic production where people gather to enjoy each other's company (Oldenburg & Brissett, 1982; Oldenburg, 1999; Soukup, 2006). From a holistic viewpoint, our results also confirm that new interaction affordances provided by media-oriented Web2.0 platforms are changing the ways in which amateur photographers or artists engage with other users. Not only do Web2.0 sites facilitate amateurs or consumers to (co)create (e.g. adding metadata), but they also enable the reproduction and distribution of content (e.g. recommending a picture to their friends) and create possibilities of consuming photographs or art in new and novel ways (e.g. through a personalized content stream enriched with metadata). Thus, Web2.0 websites are generating a new kind of media logic with regard to media consumption and production, a media logic that is expressed in the affordances of these websites.

For our respondents, Flickr and deviantART are sites, where, quietly under the surface or in full view of all, affordances are used to create spaces for engagement and community building. Both Web2.0 sites provide lots of user, document and website affordances that can serve as inter-action or social affordances. However, we noticed that these affordances are seldom used to engage in real conversations or to create an online consensus. In that respect, we also noted a lack of commitment among our respondents who indicated themselves that the quality of the dialogues is often poor. In line with Papacharissi's (2008) claim that the internet is a public space but not a public sphere, we conclude that Flickr and deviantART are public spaces. This finding emphasizes the democratic potential of Flickr and deviantART, but also points to the effort and the work needed to fulfil this potential.

In this article, we have described how Web2.0 users deploy Flickr affordances to gain access to a community of practice or a virtual third place. In that way, the practices of our respondents reflect Flickr's baseline: 'Share your photos. Watch the World'. We have also described how deviantART, 'where art meets application', represents more than just a mere 'space' where one can share amateur art. For most of our respondents, deviantART was more than a 'virtual settlement'; for them, the website acted as a 'virtual community'.

Acknowledgements

The research leading to this article was supported by IBBT (Interdisciplinary Institute for Technology). We also acknowledge Lieven De Marez and CSS's anonymous reviewers for their helpful comments on the earlier versions of the article.

References

Albrechtslund, A. (2008) Online social networking as participatory surveillance, *First Monday*. Available online at: http://www.uic.edu/htbin/cgiwrap/bin/ojs/index.php/fm/article/view/2142/1949 (accessed 20 July 2012).
Alexander, B. (2006) Web 2.0: A new wave of innovation for teaching and learning? *Educause Review*, 41(2), 33–44.

Beer, D. (2009) Power through the algorithm? Participatory web cultures and the technological unconscious, *New Media and Society*, 11(6), 985–1002.
Berg, B. L. (2001) *Qualitative research methods for the social sciences* (London, Allyn and Bacon).
Bordewijk, J. L. & van Kaam, B. (1986) Towards a new classification of teleinformation services, *Inter Media*, 14(1), 86–108.
Breslin, J. G., Passant, A. & Decker, S. (2009) *The social semantic web* (London, Springer).
Christodoulou, S. P. & Styliaras, G. D. (2008) *Digital art 2.0: Art meets web 2.0 trend*. Available online at: http://dl.acm.org/citation.cfm?id=1413667 (accessed 20 July 2012).
Conole, G. & Alevizou, P. (2010) *A literature review of the use of Web 2.0 tools in Higher Education* (Milton Keynes, Higher Education Academy).
Cox, A. (2007) Flickr: What is new in Web2.0? *Aslib Proceedings*, 60(5), 493–516.
Crawford, C. (2002) *Understanding interactivity* (San Francisco, CA, No Starch Press).
Curran, J., Fenton, N. & Freedman, D. (2012) *Misunderstanding the internet* (Abingdon, Routledge).
De Marez, L. & Schuurman, D. (2010) *Digimeter Rapport 2 Vlaanderen Wave 2 November-Maart 2010*. Available online at: http://digimeter.be/resultaten.php (accessed 20 July 2012).
De Marez, L. & Schuurman, D. (2011) *Digimeter Rapport 3 Vlaanderen Wave 3 Augustus-November 2010*. Available online at: http://digimeter.be/resultaten.php (accessed 20 July 2012).
Fontana, A. (2002) Postmodern trends in interviewing, in: J. Gubrium & J. Holstein (Eds) *Handbook of qualitative research: Context and method* (Thousand Oaks, CA, Sage), 161–175.
Fontana, A. & Frey, J. H. (2005) The interview. From neutral stance to political involvement, in: N. K. Denzin & Y. S. Lincoln (Eds) *The Sage handbook of qualitative research* (London, Sage), 695–727.
Golder, S. A. & Huberman, B. A. (2005) *The structure of collaborative tagging systems* (Ithaca, NY, Cornel University Library). Available online at: http://arxiv.org/abs/cs.DL/0508082 (accessed 20 July 2012).
Golder, S. A. & Huberman, A. (2006) Usage patterns of collaborative tagging systems, *Journal of Information Science*, 32(2), 198–208.
Hammond, T., Hannay, T., Lund, B. & Scott, J. (2005) Social bookmarking tools: A general review, *D-Lib Magazine*. Available online at: http://www.dlib.org/dlib/april05/hammond/04hammond.html (accessed 20 July 2012).
Hoegg, R., Martignoni, R., Meckel, M. & Stanoevska-Slabeva, K. (2006) *Overview of business models for web 2.0 communities*. Available online at: http://www.alexandria.unisg.ch/Publikationen/31411 (accessed 20 July 2012).
Hoem, J. (2006) Openness in communication, *First Monday*. Available online at: http://firstmonday.org/htbin/cgiwrap/bin/ojs/index.php/fm/article/view/1367/1286 (accessed 20 July 2012).
Hogan, B. J. (2009) *Networking in everyday life*. Ph.D. University of Toronto. Available online at: http://individual.utoronto.ca/berniehogan/Hogan_NIEL_10-29-2008_FINAL.pdf6 (accessed 20 July 2012).
Hudson-Smith, A., Batty, M., Crooks, A. & Milton, R. (2009) Mapping for the masses: Accessing web 2.0 through crowdsourcing, *Social Science Computer Review*, 27(4), 524–538.
Hwang, W.-Y., Hsu, J.-L., Lee, A. T., Chou, H.-W. & Lee, C.-Y. (2009) Intra-action, interaction and outeraction in blended learning environments, *Educational Technology and Society*, 11(2), 222–239.
Jakobsson, P. & Stiernstedt, F. (2010) Pirates of Silicon Valley: State of exception and dispossession in web 2.0, *First Monday*. Available online at: http://firstmonday.org/htbin/cgiwrap/bin/ojs/index.php/fm/article/view/2799/2577 (accessed 20 July 2012).
Jaokar, A. (2006) *Tim O'Reilly's seven principles of web 2.0 make a lot more sense if you change the order*, Open Gardens. Available online at: http://opengardensblog.futuretext.com/archives/2006/04/a_web_20_faq.html (accessed 20 July 2012).
Jarrett, K. (2008) Interactivity is Evil! A critical investigation of Web 2.0, *First Monday*. Available online at: http://www.uic.edu/htbin/cgiwrap/bin/ojs/index.php/fm/article/viewArticle/2140/1947 (accessed 20 July 2012).
Jensen, J. F. (1999) Interactivity: Tracking a new concept in media and communication studies, in: P. A. Meyer (Ed.) *Computer media and communication* (Oxford, Oxford University Press), 160–187.
Jensen, J. F. & Toscan, C. (Eds) (1999) *Interactive television: TV of the future or future of the TV?* (Aalborg, Aalborg University Press).
Kiousis, S. (2002) Interactivity: A concept explication, *New Media and Society*, 4(3), 355–383.
Laurent, O. (2009) Getty images targets Flickrverse, *British Journal of Photography*. Available online at: http://www.bjp-online.com/british-journal-of-photography/news/1647691/getty-images-targets-flickrverse (accessed 20 July 2012).
Leiner, D. J. & Quiring, O. (2008) What interactivity means to the user. Essential insights into and a scale for perceived interactivity, *Journal of Computer-Mediated Communication*, 14(1), 127–155.
Lewins, A. & Silver, C. (2007) *Using software in qualitative research* (London, Sage).
Lilleker, D. G. & Malagon, C. (2010) Levels of interactivity in the 2007 French presidential candidates' websites, *European Journal of Communication*, 25(1), 25–42.
Maness, J. M. (2006) Library 2.0 theory: Web 2.0 and its implications for libraries, *Webology*. Available online at: http://www.webology.org/2006/v3n2/a25.html (accessed 20 July 2012).
Marshall, M. N. (1996) Sampling for qualitative research, *Family Practice*, 13(6), 522–525.

McMillan, S. J. (2002) Exploring models of interactivity form multiple research traditions, in: L. Lievrouw & S. Livingstone (Eds) *The handbook of new media* (London, Sage), 163–175.
McMillan, S. J. & Downes, E. (2000) Defining interactivity: A qualitative identification of key dimensions, *New Media and Society*, 2(2), 157–179.
Miles, M. & Huberman, A. (1994) *Qualitative data analysis: An expanded sourcebook* (London, Sage).
Miller, P. (2005) Web 2.0: Building the new library, *Ariadne*. Available online at: http://www.ariadne.ac.uk/issue45/miller/ (accessed 20 July 2012).
Morse, J. (1998) Designing funded qualitative research, in: N. K. Denzin & Y. S. Lincoln (Eds) *Strategies of qualitative enquiry* (London, Sage), 56–85.
Nardi, B. A., Whittaker, S. & Bradner, E. (2000) *Interaction and outeraction: Instant messaging in action*. Available online at: http://dl.acm.org/citation.cfm?id=358975&bnc=1 (accessed 20 July 2012).
Newhagen, J. E. (2004) Interactivity, dynamic symbol processing, and the emergence of content in human communication, *The Information Society*, 20(5), 397–402.
Norman, D. (2002) *The design of everyday things* (New York, Basic Books).
Oldenburg, R. (1999) *The great good place: Cafes, coffee shops, bookstores, bars, hair salons and other hangouts at the heart of a community* (New York, Marlowe and Company).
Oldenburg, R. & Brissett, D. (1982) The third place, *Qualitative Sociology*, 5(4), 265–284.
O'Reilly, T. (2003) The architecture of participation, *O'Reilly Developer Weblogs*. Available online at: http://www.oreillynet.com/pub/wlg/3017 (accessed 20 July 2012).
O'Reilly, T. (2005) What is Web2.0—design patterns and business models for the next generation of software, *O'Reilly Radar*. Available online at: http://www.oreillynet.com/pub/a/oreilly/tim/news/2005/09/30/what-is-web-20.html (accessed 20 July 2012).
Papacharissi, Z. (2008) The virtual sphere 2.0, in: A. Chadwick & P. N. Howard (Eds) *Routledge handbook of internet politics* (Abingdon, Routledge), 230–245.
Patmore, C., Qureshi, H. & Nicholas, E. (2001) Consulting older community care clients about their services: Some lessons for researchers and service managers, *Research Policy and Planning*, 18(1), 4–11.
Patton, M. Q. (2002) *Qualitative research and evaluation methods* (Thousand Oaks, CA, Sage).
Petersen, S. M. (2008) Loser generated content: From participation to exploitation, *First Monday*. Available online at: http://www.uic.edu/htbin/cgiwrap/bin/ojs/index.php/fm/article/viewArticle/2141/1948 (accessed 20 July 2012).
Pissard, N. & Prieur, C. (2007) *Thematic vs. social networks in web 2.0 communities: A case study on Flickr groups*. Available online at: http://hal.inria.fr/docs/00/17/69/54/PDF/42-algotel-flickr.pdf (accessed 20 July 2012).
Prieur, C., Cardon, D., Beuscart, J.-S., Pissard, N. & Pons, P. (2008) *The strength of weak cooperation*. Available online at: http://arxiv.org/ftp/arxiv/papers/0802/0802.2317.pdf (accessed 20 July 2012).
Quiring, O. (2009) What do users associate with 'interactivity'? A qualitative study on user schemata, *New Media and Society*, 11(6), 899–920.
Rafaeli, S. (1988) Interactivity: From new media to communication, in: R. P. Hawkins, J. M. Wiemann & S. Pingree (Eds) *Advancing communication science: Merging mass and interpersonal process* (Newbury Park, CA, Sage), 110–134.
Reid, F. & Reid, D. (2010) The expressive and conversational affordances of mobile messaging, *Behaviour and Information Technology*, 29(1), 3–22.
Rigby, B. (2008) *Mobilizing generation 2.0: A practical guide to using Web 2.0 technologies to recruit, organize, and engage youth* (San Francisco, CA, John Wiley and Sons).
Rosadiuk, A. (2008) About the design and deviantART, *Synoptique*. Available online at: http://www.synoptique.ca/core/articles/s11_about_the_design/ (accessed 20 July 2012).
Scholz, T. (2008) Market ideology and the myths of web 2.0, *First Monday*. Available online at: http://www.uic.edu/htbin/cgiwrap/bin/ojs/index.php/fm/article/viewArticle/2138/1945 (accessed 20 July 2012).
Sotira, D. (2010) *Deviantart's tenth birthday*. Available online at: http://www.youtube.com/watch?v=9O2lRAooUWk (accessed 20 July 2012).
Soukup, C. (2006) Computer-mediated communication as a virtual third place: Building Oldenburg's great good places on the world wide web, *New Media and Society*, 8(3), 421–440.
Stern, A. & Wakabayashi, C. (2007) Are you ready for web2.0 marketing? *J@pan Inc.*, 72, 6–9.
Strauss, A. L. & Corbin, J. M. (1998) *Basics of qualitative research: Techniques and procedures for developing grounded theory* (Thousand Oaks, CA, Sage).
Szuprowicz, B. (1995) *Multimedia networking* (New York, McGraw-Hill).
Tremayne, M. (2008) Manipulating interactivity with thematically hyperlinked news texts: A media learning experiment, *New Media and Society*, 10(5), 703–727.
Valafar, M., Rejaie, R. & Willinger, W. (2009) *Beyond friendship graphs: A study of user interactions in Flickr*. Available online at: http://dl.acm.org/citation.cfm?id=1592672 (accessed 20 July 2012).
Zimmer, M. (2008) The externalities of search 2.0: The emerging privacy threats when the drive for the perfect search engine meets web 2.0, *First Monday*. Available online at: http://firstmonday.org/htbin/cgiwrap/bin/ojs/index.php/fm/article/view/2136/1944 (accessed 20 July 2012).

Networks for citizen consultation and citizen sourcing of expertise

Cristobal Cobo

Oxford Internet Institute, University of Oxford, Oxford, UK

This study aims to explore how public websites facilitate the creation of networks for citizen consultation. Evidence-based analysis is applied to European public-sector websites to determine the degree to which they adopt digital mechanisms and strategies to facilitate citizen participation and collaboration. This study analyses outstanding European public-sector websites as categorised by the European Commission at the 4th European eGovernment Awards (EeGA) 2009. These finalists, which were selected by independent judges, are taken as a representative sample of the range of eGovernment projects in Europe. Although other eGovernment projects with exemplary features certainly exist, the unbiased nature of this list, which consists of 52 finalists from 31 countries, provides an objective criterion for inclusion, thus making our sample analytically stronger than an opportunistic sample. The selected websites are analysed and classified based on the taxonomy of citizen participation elaborated by Dutton, who defines three levels of digital citizen engagement: (1) *sharing*, (2) *contributing*, and (3) *co-creating* knowledge. These constitute a matrix describing different levels of maturity in an e-democracy. The results of the analysis and the application of this methodology provide an overview of the strategies and policies adopted by European governments to promote and support e-democracy. Interestingly, the results also show that the vast majority of European Union (EU) public websites adopt strategies to promote only the earliest stages of digital citizen engagement, primarily at level 1. This study also reveals how the public sector utilises various tools, social networks and digital resources to create virtual networks of citizen consultation and citizen sourcing of expertise. A valuable result of this study is the taxonomy of digital citizen engagement and its operationalisation, which may be useful for future research. Finally, this work identifies practices, strategies and mechanisms for fostering e-democracy in the EU.

1. The boom in social-media networks

The emergence of the Internet, particularly social technologies, has created unprecedented mechanisms of communication and exchange, thus raising the question of how these new devices have been adopted to facilitate government-to-citizen (G2C) interactions and collaborations.

The term 'social-media tools'[1] refers to Internet services whereby users contribute to an online activity stream. Analysing social media requires one to consider how *social-media tools* and digital platforms (i.e. YouTube, Facebook, Twitter, LinkedIn) facilitate the production and dissemination of information, as well as how these platforms enable citizens to discuss and consume this information (Research Information Network, 2011).

Digital platforms such as Wikipedia, InnoCentive, YouTube and PLoS facilitate collaboration and the distributed integration of ideas between people to a remarkable extent (Cobo and Pardo 2007; Hood & Margetts, 2007; Easley & Kleinberg, 2010). However, the potential of these tools in G2C online communication (González-Bailón et al., 2010), particularly after events such as the so-called 'Arab Spring', remains a subject that must be carefully examined.

2. EU policies

High-level EU (European Union) initiatives have promoted the broad adoption of *social-media tools* that provide the opportunity to engage and participate in discussions of public interest. A relevant example can be found in the *2011–2015 European Action Plan* led by the European Commission. This action plan highlights the need to explore 'the most suitable tools and how best to apply these to effectively engage businesses, civil society and individual citizens' (European Commission, 2010, p. 7). The same document notes the need to move towards a 'more open model of design, production and delivery of online services, taking advantage of the possibility offered by collaboration between citizens, entrepreneurs and civil society' (European Commission, 2010, p. 3).

The action plan also indicates that 'empowerment means increasing the capacity of citizens, businesses and other organisations to be pro-active in society through the use of new technological tools. Public services can gain in efficiency and users in satisfaction by meeting the expectations of users better and being designed around their needs and in collaboration with them whenever possible. Empowerment also means that governments should provide easy access to public information, improve transparency and allow effective involvement of citizens and businesses in the policy-making process' (European Commission, 2010, p. 6).

One of the core ideas of this roadmap is the value of *transparency* and *citizen participation* as two enablers of this public European strategy (Etzioni, 2010). This expectation is based on the premise that individuals will make use of these platforms and their information services. At the same time, it assumes that public administrations will provide the basic conditions for increasing citizen involvement in the policy-making process.

2.1. Conceptual approximations

Can the new technology make a positive difference? Yang and Lan (2010), relying on a meta-analysis of past studies on the impact of the Internet on citizen participation in public-policy making, found that the Internet has successfully reduced the disparity in resources (primarily information and knowledge capital) between policy experts and citizens. According to these authors, reducing the gap between experts and the public promotes citizen participation in public-policy making.

Different authors (Bohman, 2004; Easley & Kleinberg, 2010) argue that the tension between experts and citizens can thus be reduced through the use of information technology. These perspectives argue that the Internet has broadened public participation because it has provided easier and cheaper access to information, fostering participatory opportunities that are more readily available through digital technologies.

Recent studies (González-Bailón *et al.*, 2010; Yang & Lan, 2010) questioning the techno-reductionist approach caution that the ability to maximise the Internet's potential for improving democratic public-policymaking lies not only in technology but also in innovations in related areas, such as education, institution-building, culture and trust-building. The authors argue that information availability is different from information perception and utilisation. Therefore, even if information is readily available on the Internet, it may be impossible for an already fragmented and non-deliberative populace to capitalise on it (Alexander & Pal, 1998).

However, the challenge seems to extend far beyond the availability of information. The goal of our research is primarily to explore to what extent and how *social-media tools* are used to facilitate collaboration and interaction between citizens and public administrations in the EU (Tolbert & McNeal, 2003).

Hardy *et al.* (2005, p. 58) note that 'although collaboration has the potential to produce powerful results, not all collaborations realize this potential. Many collaborations fail to produce innovative solutions or balance stakeholder concerns, and some even fail to generate any collective action whatsoever'. Interestingly, the authors suggest avoiding oversimplifications because collaboration between citizens does not always lead to innovative solutions.

Van Dijk (2010) acknowledges the expectation that ICTs (information and communication technologies) can empower citizens. He enquires as follows: 'Do/will ICT substantially change the relations between governments and citizens? Increases in participation and empowerment could be understood as key elements of beneficial, transformative change, but ICT can potentially also be used to curtail participation and individual freedoms' (pp. 26–27). He indicates that the 'transition is made from physical to online participation. For many years now it has been argued that online participation would be able to compensate for declining collective and institutional participation, in the way virtual communities would revitalize traditional communities. Most data show that this does not occur. ICT does not cause more political and societal interest among citizens, no higher turn-out with elections and no higher membership for political parties, trade unions or churches' (p. 21). Van Dijk, along with Hardy *et al.* (2005), Newman (2010) and Hindman (2010), states the importance of avoiding reductionist perspectives based on the idea that utilising certain technologies will ensure people's participation.

To the contrary, Zhang *et al.* (2009) suggest a distinction between civic and political participation as a consequence of social capital. According to the authors, *civic participation* refers to activities that address community concerns through non-governmental or non-electoral means, such as working on a community project. Meanwhile, *political participation* concerns activities aimed directly or indirectly at influencing the selection of elected officials and/or the development and implementation of public policy. The results of their study 'showed that reliance on social networking sites such as YouTube, Facebook and MySpace was positively related to *civic participation* but not to *political participation* or confidence in government, which was not surprising, because these social networking sites are geared toward maintaining relationships with their friends and can have the potential for stimulating community involvement' (p. 87). Despite the proximity of these concepts, it is interesting that the authors highlight how not all *social-media tools* are appropriate for all types of public engagement (Bimber, 2003; Hood & Margetts, 2007).

Castells analyses the use of *social-media tools* and their impact on political participation. He refers to the use of *social-media tools* in the crisis in the Arab world (particularly the political events that occurred in Egypt and Tunisia during early 2011). 'These popular insurrections in the Arab world constitute a turning point in the social and political history of humanity. And perhaps the most important of the internet-led and facilitated changes in all aspects of life, society, the economy and culture. And this is just the start. The movement is picking up speed, despite [the] Internet being an old technology, and deployed for the first time in 1969.' (2011). Castells, in contrast to the above authors, offers a different perspective suggesting that Internet-based technologies may constitute a turning point in the social and political history of humanity (Gibson *et al.*, 2003).

Brabham also highlights Castells' perspective regarding the relevance of digital technologies as a platform for triggering collective participation, drawing the following conclusion:

> Technology can enable deeper levels of engagement between people and governments, particularly through the medium of the Web. The crowdsourcing model, in particular, is a method for harnessing collective intellect and creative solutions from networks of citizens in organised ways that serve the needs of planners. What is needed is an embrace of the crowdsourcing model in particular and of the Web in general by the planning profession. Planning professionals and policymakers need to take risks with innovative models such as crowdsourcing. (Brabham, 2009, p. 257)

This figure, based on Caldas (2008), illustrates how the information services provided by a public administration to its citizens evolve along an S-shaped curve (see Figure 1). It also illustrates how the adoption of more complex and participatory technologies and services cannot be understood as isolated events but rather as continuous processes that include a set of socio-technological conditions that require community engagement (Chadwick, 2006). Dutton (1999, p. 193) argued that 'digital government can erode or enhance democratic processes... [but] the outcome will be determined by the

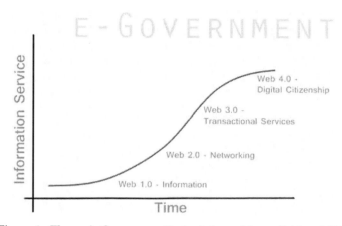

Figure 1. *Electronic Government Cycles* (adapted from Caldas, 2008)

interaction of policy choices, management strategies and cultural responses—not by advanced technology alone'. Dutton later adds that 'if organizations in the public sector wish to foster the development of CNOs [collaborative network organizations] to solve problems that they wish to be addressed, then top management must create a climate that is supportive of their development, such as by top managers recognizing the value of these initiatives or being a visible participant in them' (Dutton, 2010).

Box 1: The Global Information Technology Report 2010–2011 (Hagström, 2011, p. 91)

This global report highlights the opportunity to reinvent the government by intensifying its interaction with civil society. The document emphasises that governments must address fundamental questions regarding how to collect, analyse and exploit data. The report suggests that government agencies, departments and ministries react to the adoption of digital technologies promoting government and societal collaboration in one of three ways:

First, there are those with knee-jerk reactions, who respond by halting programs or instituting cutbacks to alleviate anxiety, even when those actions adversely affect service levels for citizens, increase unemployment, and negatively impact the country's competitiveness.

Second, there are those who take a wait-and-see approach and operate as though it is 'business as usual', waiting for a return to 'normal'. What they are not acknowledging is that the current times are the new normal and that the old times will not come back.

Third, there are leaders and organizations who view this moment in history as providing a prime opportunity for building a stronger future and preparing better systems for supporting the needs of citizens in a rapidly evolving global economy.

As seen in this compilation of perspectives, the role of ICTs in C2G interaction (between citizens and their representatives) varies significantly depending on the author's perspective. It is important, however, to realise that the *appropriate conditions* required for a network of citizens is the result of a complex integration of factors, such as information availability, the existence of adequate social tools, social capital, 'digital literacy',[2] an appropriate climate that supports public participation and an innovative model of crowdsourcing. These components are several of the basic conditions that will vary depending on the political, social and technological context (Gibson *et al.*, 2003; Chadwick, 2009).

3. Dutton's taxonomy

3.1 *Collaborative network organisations (CNOs)*

Castells (2009) explained that 'a network is a set of interconnected nodes. Nodes may be of varying relevance to the network and so particularly important nodes are called "centers"... So, networks process flows. Flows are streams of information between nodes, circulating through the channels of connection between nodes' (p. 20).

The same author adds that 'networks cooperate or compete with each other. Cooperation is based on the ability to communicate between networks. This ability depends on the existence of codes of translation and inter-operability between the networks (protocols of communication) and on access to connecting points' (p. 20).

Embracing this idea of networks as structures that facilitate the flow of collaboration, we will analyse an interpretation of networks of citizens and a taxonomy that illustrates how the flow of information benefits and affects the coordination between different nodes.

Dutton (2010) proposes that the three general ways in which CNOs utilise Internet technology are through (level 1) *sharing* documents, data and other digital objects, such as through hypertext links; (level 2) supporting collaborative *contributions*, such as through user-generated ratings and other content; and (level 3) supporting cooperative *co-creation*, such as through the group authoring of texts.

On the basis of this taxonomy, the flow of information varies depending on the stage. It ranges from the basic level (one-to-one), wherein the government 'shares' information with its citizens, to a more complex level (many-to-many), wherein citizens, among themselves or with the government, exchange information and 'co-create' content in collaboration with others.

In certain cases, platform types 1 (*sharing*), 2 (*contributing*) and 3 (*co-creating*) may overlap. This classification is useful for understanding and categorising various flows of information. These different levels of complexity may affect the creation and exchange of content among both real and virtual organisations. Adopting these categories as elaborated by Dutton *et al.* (2008, 2010) makes it possible to identify three levels of CNOs, which provide a useful framework for this field of study.

1 (Sharing): hypertextual. 'The ability to create linked documents, data and objects within a distributed network, thereby reconfiguring how and what information is shared with whom' (Dutton, 2008b, p. 11). At this level, the information can be shared, sold, or advertised.

a) *Architecture* (one-to-many): Focuses on the open sharing of documents. Uses e-mail and shared documents for the design and management of large-scale distributed projects requiring information-sharing.
b) *Openness* (open): Enables access to information through deep searching, natural-language processing, content and datasets.
c) *Control* (low): When the control of an individual's participation is low or limited and documents and data can be easily accessed, linked or searched.
d) *Modularisation* (low): Contributors have a limited level of intervention in the content (e.g. restricted ability to make changes and additions).

2 (Contributing): hypertextual—user-generated. The ability to employ *social media tools* of the Web to facilitate group communication, thereby reshaping who contributes information to the collective group, such as by enabling ratings or comments by users (tools to support collaboration and generate user content). Refers to platforms that gather and process different types of contributions.

a) *Architecture* (many-to-many): Seeks to enable user-generated content. Massive multiplayer collaborations (e.g. suggesting proposals or voting mechanisms).
b) *Openness* (networked): Access to content is based on collaborative networks (e.g. experts within a field).
c) *Control* (moderate, e.g. reputation): Management of the structure or platform is moderated and based on participation levels and reputation through peer reviews and/or consensual decision-making.
d) *Modularisation* (moderate, e.g. simple task): Modularisation maintains the task at a manageable level (e.g. aggregating and prioritising content from many individuals).

3 (Co-creating): hypertextual—user-generated—cooperative work. 'The ability for individuals to collaborate through networks that facilitate cooperative group work towards shared goals (e.g. joint writing and editing of Wikipedia), thereby reconfiguring the sequencing, composition and role of multiple contributors' (applying collaborative software to support cooperative co-creation). It attracts relevant contributors and sustains the co-creation of information products and/or services.

a) *Architecture* (many-to-many): Supports collaboration on joint products. Focuses on the collaborative production of documents and other information products (e.g. open-source software development and open 'wiki' content creation). Allows for the open production of creative artefacts.

b) *Openness* (managed): Selective. Creates a hierarchy of rights and privileges that determine who may do what within the network, enabling the administrator to configure access to key resources in numerous ways.
c) *Control* (high): High hierarchical levels of control over who participates in the network and how (e.g. a core principle governing how the community interacts).
d) *Modularisation* (high): Simplifies tasks in ways that make them manageable to the individual problem-solvers and problem-holders. Keeps tasks modular, precise and easy to complete. Provides numerous mechanisms to simplify the contributions of individuals (e.g. sub-communities of collaboration).

The combination of these concepts results in a matrix of three levels of collaboration, in which all of the referenced elements are integrated into a single scale. The aim of this matrix is to provide a basic taxonomy of collaboration wherein *sharing* is a simpler process than *contributing*, and *co-creating* is a richer and more complex level of collaboration. In addition, each one of these three levels of collaboration consists of four features: architecture, openness, control and modularisation. As seen in Table 1 numerical values have been allocated to each of these features to provide a numerical scale representative of each category.

4. Research methodology

The aims of this study:

1. To explore relevant online public initiatives from the public sector to determine whether they facilitate the creation of networks for citizen consultation and citizen-sourcing of expertise.
2. To analyse various eGovernment websites and identify the extent to which they adopt the levels of 1 (*sharing*), 2 (*contributing*) and 3 (*co-creating*) knowledge (Dutton, 2008a).
3. To identify the *social-media tools* used by European public-sector websites to facilitate the creation of networks for citizen consultation and citizen-sourcing of expertise. To review and identify relevant patterns, mechanisms and services that add value through the crowdsourcing of citizens' ideas.
4. To evaluate the usefulness of the methodology adopted in this study with respect to future research.

The key research questions:

- How are governments implementing strategies to foster online 'many-to-many' communication between citizens and public-administration bodies?
- What online mechanisms are governments adopting to incorporate crowdsourcing, the collection of ideas and 'distributed problem-solving' from citizens?

Table 1. Matrix of Collaboration

Levels of collaboration	Architecture	Value	Openness	Value	Control	Value	Modularisation	Value	Total Value
1. Sharing: Here the information can be shared, sold, or advertised. (Hypertextual)	Focus on open sharing of documents (one to many)	1	Enables access to information through deep searching (open)	1	The control of individual's participation is low or limited (low)	1	Contributors have limited level of intervention in content (low)	1	3
2. Contributing: Facilitates group communication, thereby reshaping who contributes information to the collective group (Hypertextual- User Generated)	Enables user-generated content (many-to-many).	2	Allows sharing insights, information and opinions. (networked)	2	The platform's management is based on levels of participation (moderate, reputation).	2	Modularisation keeps the task at a manageable level (moderate, simple task).	2	6
3. Co-creating: Allows attracting and sustaining relevant contributors and the co-creation of information products and services. (Hypertextual- User Generated – Cooperative Work)	Allows collaborative production of information products (many-to-many).	3	Creates a hierarchy of rights and privileges (managed).	3	Hierarchical levels of control over who participates and how (high).	3	Keeping tasks modular, precise and easy to complete (high).	3	9

- Are online public platforms a relevant space for facilitating discussions and collaboration from citizen to citizen?
- Does the current use of G2C online technologies foster 'user-generated content'? If so, how is such content shared with citizens?

4.1 *Sampling criteria*

The websites analysed in this study were finalists in the European eGovernment Awards Consortium (EeGA) (Commission of the European Communities, 2009)[3] as determined by independent judges. They were selected from this competition as a representative sample of the range of eGovernment projects in Europe. Although other eGovernment projects exist, many of which have exemplary features, the unbiased nature of this list provides an objective criterion for inclusion, making our sample analytically stronger than an opportunistic sample. An opportunistic sample based on the quality of the websites would not be sufficient to identify the more remarkable cases highlighted by the European Commission. The analytical sample was based on the selection criteria followed by the EeGA, which resulted in a comprehensive and consistent sample in terms of characteristics (i.e. public sector), geographical location (i.e. European governments) and timeframe (i.e. 2009). Moreover, the selection was made by independent experts from a variety of backgrounds from across Europe to ensure the widest possible coverage in terms of specialist knowledge and geographical balance. The sample consists of 52 finalists from 31 countries.[4]

EUBestPractices (Box 2)

4th European eGovernment Awards 2009 (www.epractice.eu/awards)
The *European eGovernment Awards* is a European Commission initiative organised *every two years that coincides* with the biannual high-level EU Ministerial eGovernment conference. The aim is to identify and select good examples of the use of ICT in public services and to highlight the benefits of ICT to society, including:

- Improved quality of life of citizens
- Increased public trust in government
- Increased competitiveness for European enterprises

The purpose of the European eGovernment Awards is to support the implementation of European eGovernment policies and action plans within the wider framework of information society policies and strategies (eEurope or i2010), to support the Open Method of Coordination (OMC) and to support the overall objectives of the Lisbon Agenda of promoting growth and jobs in the European Union. In this context, the Awards play a major role in the European

Commission's good practice exchange initiative in the field of eGovernment.

The 4th edition of the prestigious European eGovernment Awards aimed to promote good practices and innovative electronic solutions developed by public authorities across Europe. These practices are meant to facilitate citizens' and businesses' access to public services, to reduce administrative burdens and to increase the efficiency of public administrations. All finalists competing in the Awards used state-of-the-art applications such as innovative websites and portals, SMS-based services, Web 2.0 and other ICT-based solutions. A panel of independent experts from a variety of backgrounds drawn from across Europe, ensuring the widest possible coverage in terms of specialist knowledge and geographical balance, was commissioned to evaluate all entries submitted to the European eGovernment Awards 2009. Out of 259 submissions from **31 countries, 52 cases were** shortlisted as finalists (Commission of the European Communities, 2009).

The following **categories** were covered by the Awards:

- **eGovernment supporting a single market (5 cases):** The most outstanding cross-border eServices and information-sharing practices that impact the mobility of citizens and businesses across the EU are[-included] in this category. A candidate should deal with the implementation and/or support of internal market policies such as the Services Directive, employment policies, public procurement, or social security systems.
- **eGovernment empowering citizens (18 cases):** The focus here is to identify the most outstanding practices facilitating access to public services for citizens as the major beneficiaries of eGovernment. ICT solutions for the participation, engagement and/or involvement of all groups in society in policy-making; implementation and public-service provision are included in this category.
- **eGovernment empowering businesses (6 cases):** The focus here is to identify the most outstanding practices at improving and creating easier access to public services for companies. Cases in this category support the creation of business opportunities (potentially across Europe), thereby enhancing competition and generating savings for businesses and in particular, small and medium enterprises (SMEs).
- **eGovernment enabling administrative efficiency and effectiveness (23 cases):** The most outstanding practices at innovating and/or reorganising services and processes that improve the efficiency and effectiveness of administrations and reduce administrative burdens are[included] in this category.

Table 2. Classification of websites based on the values described in Table I

Criteria used in cases of overlap or a combination of features from different levels
Websites at level **1. Sharing**: Hypertextual (with no more than one feature from another level)
Websites at level **2. Contributing**: Hypertextual-User-Generated (with two or more features of this level)
Websites at level **3. Co-creating**: Hypertextual-User-Generated- Cooperative Work (with two or more features of this level). Also included in this category are those sites with at least two features from the previous level.

5. The matrix and methodology used to analyse online collaboration between citizens

The elaboration of this matrix is supported by previous empirical research in the field of distributed problem-solving networks (David, 2008; Dutton, 2008a; Dutton et al., 2008). In this study, this matrix was adapted to operationalise and describe the different levels of G2C in the field of citizen-sourcing of expertise. We adopted the conceptualisation of Dutton et al. (2008) to describe three levels of collaborative networks. In addition, these levels consisted of four features: architecture, openness, control and modularisation.

The matrix presented above was used to analyse and categorise the websites included in this study (the 52 finalists in the EeGA). It is important to note that some of the websites in this analysis include features from multiple categories (overlapping features). For instance, website 'X' has 'architecture' and 'openness', which are included in level 1 (*sharing*). At the same time, the values of 'control' and 'modularisation', as described in website 'X', are better represented by the description provided for level 2 (*contributing*). To provide an inclusive but consistent classification, Table 2 provides details of the criteria used to rank the websites (particularly in cases of overlap).

6. Results

6.1 Descriptions of the five highest-ranked websites

A ranking of the reviewed platforms was developed after visiting and categorising each of the awarded websites (52 finalists in the EeGA). The classification and ranking for each of these websites can be found at the following URL: https://docs.google.com/spreadsheet/ccc?key=0AmBXUpZP05UodG5vUWlTU1dLVVNxREdFcGxLT2VTU1E&hl=es#gid=0.

The aim of this ranking was to identify those platforms that reached a higher level in terms of collaboration between citizens and public networking (according to the values described in Table 1 and 3).

Table 3. Classification of websites based on the values described in Table I

Criteria used in cases of overlap or a combination of features from different levels	Number of websites	Total Average
Sites at level **1. Sharing**	40	76.9
Sites at level **2. Contributing**	4	7.7
Sites at level **3. Co-creating**	5	9.6
Not enough information or inactive	3	5.8
Total	52	100

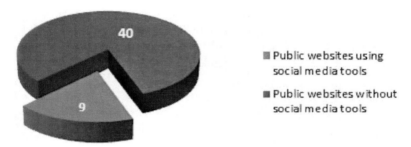

Figure 2. The number of websites adopting *social-media tools* within their platforms

Of the 52 European public-sector website finalists included in this study, only 49 of were active and provided public information (February 2011). After reviewing those 49 websites and analysing them using the taxonomy and criteria described in Tables 1 and 2, 40 websites were found to beat level 1 (*sharing*), 4 were at level 2 (*contributing*) and only 5 were at level 3 (*co-creating*) (see Figure 2).

The presence of 'external channels of participation' (*social-media tools*) was identified in only eight public websites (16.3%) (see Figure 3). Table 4 identifies the external *social-media tools* included among the analysed public platforms.

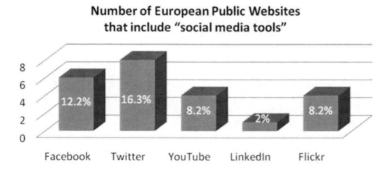

Figure 3. The frequency with which *social-media tools* appear in public websites

Table 4. Social Media Tools used in the EU public websites

Social Media Tool	Number of websites that include social media tools	Average among all websites in the study that include social media tools
Facebook	6	12.2
Twitter	8	16.3
YouTube	4	8.2
LinkedIn	1	2.0
Flickr	4	8.2

Once the platforms were analysed, the five highest-ranked websites were identified and examined. A summary of these websites is presented here. This summary is the result of a qualitative description of those features that facilitate the creation and maintenance of 'networks for citizen consultation'.

---

e-Catalunya: boosting eGov innovation by Communities of Practice
http://ecatalunya.gencat.net (Spain)
12 Total value assigned based on the CNO classification (see Table 1)

This website is an initiative of the Government of Catalonia (Spain) that promotes citizen dialogue and exchanges of experiences. The information provided in the website is organised into thematic groups. This platform offers multiple easy channels of communication and participation that facilitate the sharing of knowledge, the creation of communities of interest and collective discussions on topics of common interest (architecture). e-Catalunya does not provide links to external *social-media tools* because all of the transactions are generated within the site. Once the user has logged in to one community or group, s/he becomes part of a self-organised process of participation (control). The variety of topics and the tools of participation (i.e. photo albums, blogs, calendars, forums, mailing lists, wikis and collective surveys) illustrate the diversity of channels and the high level of modularisation. The user's participation is sufficiently individualised and flexible to allow for different types of interaction: 'one-to-many', 'many-to-many', C2C ('citizen-to-citizen', or interactions among citizens) or C2G. There is no visible evidence of centralisation (control) or editorial management in the dialogue and interaction between the participants. However, because e-Catalunya does not include any external social-media tools, all of the data and the transactions are registered and hosted by the public entity.

Architecture (Value #3): The platform fosters many-to-many communication. *Openness* (Value #3): The creation of networks on the platform is based on customisable and adaptable structures. *Control* (Value #3): Participants have a high level of control over how the community interacts. *Modularisation* (Value #3): Participation is simplified through mechanisms that facilitate collaboration.

PloneGov: open-source collaboration for the public sector
www.plonegov.org (Belgium)
12 Total value assigned based on the CNO classification (see Table 1)

PloneGov (Belgium) is an open-source community that collaborates in the creation of online services and platforms for the public sector. The aim of this initiative is to facilitate the transfer of knowledge regarding the creation of websites for public organisations and to enhance the participation of citizens in the government policy decision-making process. Plone provides an ecosystem of collaboration through the participation of sub-communities. These sub-communities are grouped according to the cultural, geographical or thematic preferences of the participants (high level of openness and modularisation). The participants are invited to add content and edit through an online workflow whereby different users have different roles. This tool helps to eliminate the duplication of efforts between localities through sharing and collaboration. In addition, public organisations and open-source communities can access and exchange resources of common interest. The collaboration includes computer-based decision-support tools such as agendas, newsletters, RSS feeds, geo-location and a mini website for companies and associations.
The primary contribution of this 'back office' initiative is that it fosters what can be called a 'meta-collaboration'. In other words, it provides tools, expertise and resources to facilitate *many-to-many* collaborations and citizen-sourcing between various governments around the world (not restricted to the EU).

Architecture (Value #3): The platform enhances communication between hundreds of sub-communities. *Openness* (Value #3): Clear hierarchies of rights and privileges empower management and decision-making. *Control* (Value #3): The platform gives all users autonomy without affecting coordination between different networks. *Modularisation* (Value #3): A variety of tools are provided to facilitate collective problem-solving.

Participa en Andalucía—CFRPA
www.participaenandalucia.net (Spain)
10 Total value assigned based on the CNO classification (see Table 1)

'Participa en Andalucía' (Spain) is a platform that promotes and facilitates public participation in various aspects of public life. The platform was conceived as an instrument whereby citizens can propose, exchange and promote ideas. It includes a voting system through which citizens can submit initiatives and vote for others' ideas. After a selection process (determined by public voting), a coordination committee of the local government reviews the proposals and assesses their viability (control). This tool enhances C2C and C2G interactions. The process is clearly described (rights and duties of citizens) and provides a transparent workflow of the citizens' proposals. 'Participa en Andalucía' enables direct interaction between citizens and their local representatives, thereby promoting political engagement and participation in matters of public interest. The platform is linked to Facebook and Twitter, allowing the citizens to disseminate their ideas and opinions publicly through various media.

Interestingly, this platform adopts a different strategy than the one implemented by e-Catalunya. In this case, the content and transactions promoted through the public platforms are linked and expanded through external *social-media tools*.

Architecture (Value #2): The website supports and promotes collective user-content generation. *Openness* (Value #2): Networks of collaboration are boosted through the adoption of participatory tools. *Control* (Value #3): Taxonomies and principles of participation are clearly stipulated. *Modularisation* (Value #3): Mechanisms for contributing are provided and clearly distinguished.

Interoperability Infrastructure for Service Transformation
www.ermis.gov.gr (Greece)
10 Total value assigned based on the CNO classification (see Table 1)

Ermis (Greece) is a platform that aims to facilitate dialogue and exchange between citizens. It provides an interoperability framework that covers more than 18,000 public-administration entities. Through Ermis, the government provides a central source of comprehensive information for citizens and businesses. Moreover, this is a platform that allows citizens to suggest and discuss ideas, opinions and matters of public interest. The citizens can also rank and comment on the quality (usefulness) of the information provided by public organisations. Users can browse the website anonymously, but authentication is a prerequisite for participating in public forums. In addition, registered users can participate through multiple tools, such as posting public questions, publishing comments or suggestions, participating in surveys or polls and even ranking the comments of other contributors. This tool also highlights popular topics and discussions.

One of the most attractive aspects of this platform is the 'transparency' of participation, which allows citizens to have an active role in matters of public interest. The tool provides high levels of participation by encouraging citizens to post questions, suggestions, complaints and/or proposals publicly (instead of in a black box, as in other cases). With this tool, others can add or co-create content based on previous contributions.

Architecture (Value #2): This platform supports massive multiplayer collaboration. *Openness* (Value #2): Opinions and contributions are supported through a variety of networks and organisations. *Control* (Value #3): Different means to administrate participation and contribution are provided. *Modularisation* (Value #3): Participants find tasks to be modular, precise and simple to accomplish.

Cologne—Participatory Budgeting
buergerhaushalt.stadt-koeln.de (Germany)
9 Total value assigned based on the CNO classification (see Table 1)

'Buergerhaushalt' is an online platform designed by the government of Cologne (Germany) to create a participatory budget in matters related to 'environmental protection' and 'education and training'. Although the platform is not currently active, it remains online. In 2009, users were invited to submit and evaluate the pros and cons of ideas suggested by the community. Any visitor could upload suggestions to the platform. Moreover, to evaluate and comment on proposals, users needed to register with a valid e-mail address. Participation included a process of discussion and competition for the best suggestions submitted by citizens. The platform was administered by a team that ensured that the rules were followed and that a fair dialogue was maintained throughout the process. The first (highest-rated) 100 citizens' proposals (for each of the two above-mentioned topics) were audited by the administrators and submitted to the Council of the City of Cologne. In addition, this entity evaluated the proposals and published a public deliberation of the viability of these initiatives. The use of this website was not restricted to the residents of Cologne. All people interested in participating were permitted to join this dialogue.

Architecture (Value #2): User-generated content mechanisms are provided within the platform. *Openness* (Value #2): The content is organised and administered based on networks of collaboration. *Control* (Value #2): The platform supplies peer-review and consensual decision-making tools. *Modularisation* (Value #3): Mechanisms for contribution are provided and clearly distinguished.

7. Conclusions

The adoption of *social-media tools* among public-service websites is not synonymous with citizen participation or transparency. As described earlier, a complex network of components exists, including information availability, adequate social tools, social capital and digital literacy, each of which contributes to the creation of a climate that facilitates public participation.

Using *social-media tools* as a shortcut to foster citizen involvement can generate unanticipated outcomes. However, if we consider that Facebook and Twitter have over 750 and 200 million registered users, respectively (New York Times, 2011), the modest adoption of these platforms by the public sector is illustrative of the 'digital agora' and the behaviour of European public administrations within the digital landscape.

Considering Hagström's (2011) observations of how governments adopt digital technologies to interact with society, it is important for governments to comprehend and assess the importance of these mechanisms for communicating with their constituents. Therefore, in addition to selecting a particular technology, device or *social-media tool*, it is important that public administrations be able to design their strategies, channels and mechanisms to interact in a way that promotes trust and collaboration within different sectors of society according to a specific context. A discussion of the study's main results is presented here.

i. *A majority of 'Sharing' websites*: This study identified a considerable amount of *sharing* websites that offer limited levels of intervention from the citizens' perspective. In terms of the level of collaboration in the 49 selected active websites, 40 (76.9%) were classified as (1) *sharing*, 4 (7.7%) were classified as (2) *contributing* and only 5 (9.6%) were classified as (3) *co-creating*. On the basis of a review of the finalists' websites (EeGA), a significant majority of the 'awarded' public websites adopted the lowest level of collaboration and interaction.

ii. *Infrequent use of mechanisms fostering participation:* Despite the growing awareness of collaborative platforms and the relevance of *social-media tools* as described in the *EU 2011–2015 Action Plan*, our study indicates that the adoption of 'many-to-many' tools to foster collaboration between citizens is a phenomenon that remains in its early stages. On the basis of this unbiased sample, the adoption of digital platforms was not identified as a relevant aspect among the awarded public-sector websites (EeGA). This aspect suggests a miscellaneous range of priorities adopted by different EU public digital platforms.

iii. *Basic mechanisms of interactivity:* Despite the proliferation of tools to facilitate online communication and interaction, most of the analysed websites included only traditional channels of information. Interestingly, a review of the websites found that e-mail (or online forms in the 'contact' section) and telephone are still the primary channels offered for interacting with the government. 'One-to-one' channels have been more widely adopted than 'one-to-many' or 'many-to-many' channels. In addition, little real-time interaction was observed (virtually none of the websites included real-time chat or other synchronous communication tools). On the basis of this review, the analysed websites demonstrate a preference for traditional communication channels.

iv. *No guarantee of citizen participation:* If a public website is expected to provide added value, it should implement channels and tools that facilitate citizen 'co-creation' (Dutton *et al.*, 2008; Dutton, 2010). Nevertheless, it is also important to consider that the inclusion of these tools is only one step towards facilitating public collaboration. By no means can the mere inclusion of social-networking platforms be seen as a guarantee of citizen participation; much work has yet to be done to facilitate and foster public collaboration. The significant number of platforms that provide limited levels of information-exchange (76.9% of the websites analysed in this study) reveals a potential gap between regional EU policies and the implementation of these strategies among public websites.

v. *Outsourcing collaboration:* The diversity of strategies for embracing *social-media tools* proved instructive. Some platforms are adapting external technologies and services, whereas others are developing these tools for themselves (for instance, e-Catalunya). Additional observations include the following:

vi. a. The number of websites that have embedded *social-media tools* is low. The most popular tool was Twitter (on only eight of the reviewed sites) followed by Facebook (on only six).

b. Websites that adopt *social-media tools* are considered to be 'intensive users'. In other words, the use of these tools is highly concentrated within a small number of public websites.

c. The incorporation of these external channels of participation (*social-media tools*) is seen as a strategy for outsourcing (or externalising) public collaboration. In cases where channels fostered citizens' dialogue and collaboration, public administrations tended to externalise those exchanges by way of private companies (for instance, Facebook or Twitter). The outsourcing of communications with and between citizens offers potential benefits, such as familiarity with these tools, the visibility and reliability of these platforms and virtually no requirement of investment or non-technical support. However, if public services rely on external national or international companies with private interests and regulations, there is a risk of compromising participants' privacy.

vii. *Further research:* The findings of this study suggest that it is important to explore not only the different causes underlying the low adoption of *social-media tools* but also the reason for the high concentration of these collaborative tools on a small number of websites. This finding raises new questions regarding the familiarity (digital literacy) of those who design and administer communications between public services, citizens and companies. Further research is needed to identify the motivations and strategies of those who administer these types of public platforms. Research is also needed to develop new studies that explore and evaluate the usefulness of incorporating these *social-media tools* into C2G interactions.

viii. *Methodology:* The levels of digital collaboration described in the collaborative matrix (Table I) and its taxonomy are useful and replicable methodological approaches that can be adopted in future studies. This novel methodology was a useful approach for categorising, qualifying and understanding different flows of information-exchange and also for determining the strengths and weaknesses of different online platforms.

8. Limitations of the study

The study relies on selected websites included in the European eGovernment Awards (European Commission). This initiative may not be fully representative of all

European public-sector websites. The awards' selection process may have created a bias in the sample. Further research will be necessary to identify the most representative platforms that foster 'citizen-distributed problem-solving'. Another limitation of this study is that some of the platforms provided reduced access to the information (requiring ID middleware, cryptographic keys, restrictions to specific communities or IP control). Such restrictions made deeper analysis of certain websites included in this study more challenging.

Acknowledgements

This study was supported through the Knetworks project (Knowledge Dissemination Network for the Atlantic Area) and in collaboration with the Socio-Economic Services for European Research Project (SESERV).

Notes

1. Although there are other largely synonymous terms for such services (such as Web 2.0, participatory media and social networking platforms), for consistency, this document will use the terms 'social-media tools' to describe the technologies and applications that facilitate participatory information-sharing, interoperability, user-centred design and collaboration on the World Wide Web (Wikipedia, 2010).
2. Regarding 'digital literacy', Buckingham (2007, p. 53) asserts, 'The increasing convergence of contemporary media means that we need to be addressing the skills and competencies–the multiple literacies–that are required by the whole range of contemporary forms of communication'.
3. These platforms have been qualified as the best practices in the EU and are able to provide innovative electronic solutions that facilitate citizen access to public services, reduce administrative burdens and increase the efficiency of public administrations.
4. A list of websites is available via the following link: https://docs.google.com/spreadsheet/ccc?key=0AmBXUpZP05UodG5vUWlTU1dLVVNxREdFcGxLT2VTU1E&hl=es#gid=0

References

Alexander, C. J. & Pal, L. A. (1998) *Digital democracy: policy and politics in the wired world* (Toronto, Oxford University Press).
Bimber, B. A. (2003) *Information and American democracy: technology in the evolution of political power* (Cambridge, Cambridge University Press).
Bohman, J. (2004) Expanding dialogue: the Internet, the public sphere and prospects for transnational democracy, *The Editorial Board of the Sociological Review*, 52(1), 131–135.
Brabham, D. C. (2009) Crowdsourcing the public participation process for planning projects, *Planning Theory*, 8(3), 242–262. Available online at: http://plt.sagepub.com/content/8/3/242.short (accessed 11 April 2011).
Buckingham, D. (2007) Digital media literacies: rethinking media education in the age of the Internet, *Research in Comparative and International Education*, 2(1), 43–55.
Caldas, A. (2008) *Do i-Government ao c-Government O Papel do GovernonaPromoção da InovaçãoTecnológica e nasRedes de Cooperação. Seminario de capitalizacioninvestigacion, desarrollo e innovacion.* Universidade da

Coruña, Spain. Available online at: http://www.fundacion.udc.es/seminario-sudoe-innovacion/docs/2102/A_Caldas.pdf (accessed 11 April 2011).

Castells, M. (2009) *Communication power* (Oxford, Oxford University Press).

Castells, M. (2011) *The popular uprisings in the Arab world perhaps constitute the most important internet-led and facilitated change*, Universitat Oberta de Catalunya (UOC). Available online at: http://www.uoc.edu/portal/english/sala-de-premsa/actualitat/entrevistes/2011/manuel_castells.html (accessed 11 April 2011).

Chadwick, A. (2006) *Internet politics: states, citizens, and new communication technologies* (New York, Oxford University Press).

Chadwick, A. (2009) *Routledge handbook of Internet politics* (New York, Taylor & Francis).

Commission of the European Communities, Information Society and Media Directorate-General (2009) *4th European eGovernment Awards: Exhibition Catalogue. Commission of the European Communities*, Available online at: http://www.epractice.eu/files/download/mediakit/exhcat2009.pdf.

Cobo, R. C. & Pardo, K. H. (2007) *Planeta Web 2.0.* Inteligenciacolectiva o medios fast food (México, Flacso).

David, P. A. (2008) *Toward an analytical framework for the study of distributed problem-solving networks*, Unpublished manuscript. Available online at: http://papers.ssrn.com/sol3/papers.cfm?abstract_id=1302927 (accessed 23 February 2011).

Dutton, W. H. (1999) *Society on the line: information politics in the digital age* (Oxford and New York, Oxford University Press).

Dutton, W. H. (2008a) The wisdom of collaborative network organizations: capturing the value of networked individuals, *Prometheus: Critical Studies in Innovation*, 26(3), 211–230.

Dutton, W. H. (2008b) *Collaborative network organizations: new technical, managerial and social infrastructures to capture the value of distributed intelligence*. OII DPSN Working Paper No. 5. Available online at: http://ssrn.com/abstract=1302893 (accessed 23 February 2011).

Dutton, W. (2010) *Networking distributed public expertise: strategies for citizen sourcing advice to government*. Occasional Paper Series in Science & Technology, Science and Technology Policy Institute (STPI) Institute for Defence Analyses. Available online at: https://www.ida.org/stpi/occasionalpapers/papers/OP-3-2010-NetworkingDistributed%20PublicExpertise-v2.pdf (accessed 23 February 2011).

Dutton, W. H., David, P. A. & Richter, W. (2008) *The performance of distributed problem solving networks: a final report on the OII-MTI project*. Unpublished manuscript. Available online at: http://papers.ssrn.com/sol3/papers.cfm?abstract_id=1302923 (accessed 23 February 2011).

Easley, D. & Kleinberg, J. (2010) *Networks, crowds, and markets: reasoning about a highly connected world* (New York, Cambridge University Press).

European Commission (2010) Commission Communication: *The European eGovernment Action Plan 2011–2015, Harnessing ICT to promote smart, sustainable & innovative Government*. European Commission (Information Society and Media). Available online at: http://ec.europa.eu/information_society/activities/egovernment/action_plan_2011_2015/docs/action_plan_en_act_part1_v2.pdf (accessed 23 February 2011).

Etzioni, A. (2010) Is transparency the best disinfectant? *Journal of Political Philosophy*, 18(4), 389–404.

Gibson, R. K., Nixon, P. & Ward, S. (2003) *Political parties and the Internet: net gain?* (London, Routledge).

González-Bailón, S., Kaltenbrunner, A. & Banchs, R. E. (2010) The structure of political discussion networks: a model for the analysis of online deliberation, *Journal of Information Technology*, 25(2), 230–243.

Hagström, M. (2011) Transformation 2.0 for an effective social strategy, in: S. Duttaand & I. Miaeds (Eds) *The Global Information Technology Report 2010–2011*. Geneve, INSEAD & World Economic Forum, pp. 91–98. Available online at: http://www3.weforum.org/docs/WEF_GITR_Report_2011.pdf (accessed 16 August 2011).

Hardy, C., Lawrence, T. B. & Grant, D. (2005) Discourse and collaboration: the role of conversations and collective identity, *The Academy of Management Review*, 30(1), 58–77.

Hindman, M. (2010) *The myth of digital democracy* (Princeton, NJ, Princeton University Press).

Hood, C. C. & Margetts, H. Z. (2007) *The tools of government in the digital age: (public policy and politics)* (London, Palgrave Macmillan).

New York Times (2011) *Business—Companies*. The New York Times Company. Available online at: http://topics.nytimes.com/topics/news/business/companies/index.html (accessed 2 August 2011).

Newman, M. E. J. (2010) *Networks: an introduction* (Oxford, Oxford University Press).

Research Information Network (2011) *Social media: A guide for researchers*. International Centre for Guidance Studies. Available online at: http://www.rin.ac.uk/our-work/communicating-and-disseminating-research/social-media-guide-researchers (accessed 16 August 2011).

The European eGovernment Action Plan 2011–2015 (2010) *Harnessing ICT to promote smart, sustainable & innovative Government*. Brussels, 15 December 2010. Available online at: http://ec.europa.eu/information_society/activities/egovernment/action_plan_2011_2015/docs/action_plan_en_act_part1_v2.pdf (accessed 16 August 2011).

Tolbert, C. J. & McNeal, R. S. (2003) Unravelling the effects of the Internet on political participation? *Political Research Quarterly*, 56(2), 175–185.

Van Dijk, J. (2010) *Study on the social impact of ICT. EC*. Available online at: http://ec.europa.eu/information_society/eeurope/i2010/docs/eda/social_impact_of_ict.pdf (accessed 16 August 2011).

Wikipedia contributors (2010) 'Web 2.0', *Wikipedia, The Free Encyclopedia*. Available online at: http://en.wikipedia.org/w/index.php?title=Web_2.0&oldid=445095502 (accessed 16 August 2011).

Yang, L. & Lan, Z. G. (2010) Internet's impact on expert-citizen interactions in public policymaking—a meta-analysis, *Government Information Quarterly*, 27(4), 431–441.

Zhang, W. *et al.* (2010) The revolution will be networked, *Social Science Computer Review*, 28(1), 75–92.

The political economy of information production in the Social Web: chances for reflection on our institutional design

Vasilis Kostakis
Tallinn University of Technology, Tallinn, Estonia

This paper is based on the idea that information production on the Web is mainly taking place within either proprietary- or Commons-based platforms. The productive processes of those two 'workplaces' of information production do share some certain characteristics, but they also have several crucial differences. These two modes of production are discussed here and it is investigated how production is organised in each case. In addition, the paper concludes by articulating the lessons taught by the investigation of the structural relationships of information production for enhancing modern societies' institutional design.

Introduction

The idea that the main body of information production on the Social Web is taking place within either proprietary- or Commons-based platforms is used in this paper as a point of departure. The purpose of this paper is to discuss this seemingly contradictory distinction, focusing on the common characteristics as well as the essential differences of these two modes of production, and it argues that the lessons taught by the investigation of their differences can be of a particular interest to social policy. To become more specific, it is articulated that what sets Commons-based peer production apart from the proprietary-based mode of production—the 'industrial one', according to Benkler (2006)—is its mode of governance and property, whose foundation stones are the abundance of resources, openness, commons ownership and the underestimated, from the Standard Textbooks Economics theories, power of meaningful human cooperation that delivers innovative results, such as the Mozilla Firefox browser, BIND (the most widely used DNS software) or Sendmail (the router of the majority of email). This paper's narrative begins with some succinct definitions of the central concepts to the discussion that follows. It is then described how the information production in both proprietary-based and Commons-based platforms is organised, arguing that the latter mode inaugurates an alternative path of economic development—building on Bauwens' (2005a, 2005b) triptych of peer production, governance and property. Concluding, it is claimed that the processes of Commons-based peer production can offer interesting insights for a more productive and meaningful institutional design of the modern, information-based societies while new technological capabilities, such as desktop manufacturing, are developing.

Why 'information production'?

In the present context, the term 'political economy of information production' connotes the study of the structural relationships of information production and how they can affect political institutions and outcomes. In other words, the processes of production, distribution and consumption of information and their relation with law, culture and social policy are all put under examination. Particularly, the focus is on the production that is happening with the aid of the so-called Web 2.0, Read/Write Web or Social Web, which facilitates the ground for user-generated content (Benkler, 2006).

It is important to highlight that although the concept of 'information production' does not explicitly refer to the processes of consumption and distribution, here the aforementioned term is related to all of them. This is so for numerous reasons. Following Karl Marx's work—centrally *Das Kapital I* (1867) and its basis the *Grundrisse* (1858) (Marx, 1992, 1993)—we become familiar with the significant impact of the relations of production to the formation of the socio-economic reality, which at least as a heuristic insight about the causes and consequences of the social living-together has not lost its interpretative utility today. Moreover, in *Grundrisse*, Marx argues that the typical value chain, which includes the processes of production ('the generality'), distribution ('the particularity') and consumption ('the singularity'), is 'admittedly a coherence, but a shallow one' (Marx, 1993, p. 89): things are much more complex than they seem, especially in immaterial production.

Information is circular, in the sense that it is both input and output (in order to write a paper, other papers are required) to its own production (Benkler, 2006), therefore it becomes very difficult to distinguish production, distribution and consumption of information. Actually these processes are completely interwoven: the 'value chain is transformed to the point of being entirely unrecognizable' (Bruns, 2008, p. 21). For instance, in the ecology of information Commons, there is a 'seemingly endless string of users' who act incrementally as content producers and gradually extend and improve the information present in it (Bruns, 2008, p. 21). As Bruns (2008, p. 21) writes, 'whether in this chain participants act more as users ... or more as producers varies over time and across tasks; overall they take on a hybrid user/producer role which inextricably interweaves both forms of participation'. Hence, the traditional understanding of production becomes rather a particular branch of production, with information production as a social body that is active 'in a greater or a sparser totality of branches of production' (Marx, 1993, p. 86).

The Social Web and participatory platforms

'Social Web', 'Read/Write Web' or 'Web 2.0' are terms that refer to a relatively new set of Internet applications that facilitate user-generated content and use certain media-producing technologies, such as HTML5, CSS 2.0 and Ajax, which make Web services (in combination with the advancement of Internet connections) lighter and faster. These technologies contribute to the functionality of the Web, transforming it into a smooth navigation, interaction and production platform (Porter, 2008; Kostakis, 2009). The present paper prefers the term 'Social Web', as it addresses better the social character of the participatory architecture which is a result of the cumulative changes that those technologies enabled. According to O'Reilly (2006), the Social Web induces social creativity, collaboration and information-sharing among users, who can own data on a site and exercise control over it. It gave rise to several business ventures such as Facebook, Flickr, MySpace and YouTube, which generate huge profits. For instance, in October 2007, Microsoft bought 1.6% of Facebook for US$246 million, and a year later, Google Inc. reached a deal to acquire YouTube for US$1.65 billion (Kostakis, 2009). These proprietary-based, but participatory, platforms create sharing/aggregation economies that are not Commons-oriented. Users share or contribute information, which can be either a product of their own or just someone else's creation, most of the time with non-monetary motives such as enjoyment, recognition, reputation and knowledge (Benkler, 2011). However, generally speaking, they do not directly or consciously participate in order to create common products: they are not part of a certain project that follows certain rules and has set goals to produce relatively clearly defined results in an ecology of common ownership, as happens in Wikipedia or in Free/Open Source Software (FOSS) projects. Platform owners make money from the aggregated attention function, mainly through advertising (for example, MySpace) or based on the Freemium model (for example, Flickr), as explained by Anderson (2009), or in other cases they exploit the collective intelligence for their interests. The latter is well-summarised in Howe's (2006) words—'it's not outsourcing; it's crowdsourcing'—in a *Wired* article that brings to the fore cases from the network television market to companies such as Procter & Gamble or Boeing. A combination of the aforementioned practices or other innovative (for example, think of eBay, which is actually an intermediary that creates markets by enabling and exploiting users' interactions, or of Amazon, which is an e-shop with integrated participatory technologies) or traditional models (for instance, a typical e-seller) are also possible. On the other hand, the Social Web technologies and the Internet in general have given rise to the sphere of information Commons; think of FOSS (Ubuntu, Mozilla Firefox, BIND, Sendmail, Apache, etc.) or Wikipedia. Those projects are developed around communities of users on Commons-based platforms, which are quite autonomous, and their results belong to the Commons pool. Nevertheless, under certain conditions, those communities appreciate the involvement of for-profit entities as they can offer support and thus strengthen the Commons sphere (Bauwens, 2005a, 2005b, 2007). In the next two sections, the processes of information production within both proprietary-based and Commons-based platforms are described in more detail.

Proprietary-based platforms

Graham (cited in Kleiner & Wyrick, 2007) states that there are mainly three roles one can assume in the Web: the professional user, who is an advanced participant in Web production with monetary incentives, amongst others; the amateur user, who plays a significant role, especially in proprietary-based platforms' production (and who is discussed here in detail); and the final user, who is not eager to take part directly in Web production and just distributes and/or consumes information. Two other categories can be added: that of the benevolent 'white hat' hacker, who, following Wark's (2004) and Levy's (2001) spirit, carries some characteristics of the professional (i.e. profound and specialised knowledge) and some of the amateur (i.e. participation on a non-profit basis, mostly induced by motives such as knowledge, communication, romanticism or reputation; it can be either some or all of them); and that of the malicious 'black hat' hacker who has criminal intentions.

In the years of the early Web, amateur users, i.e. those who were willing to participate in the production but who lacked the necessary knowledge to handle the convoluted means of production, were incapable of producing mainly due to the early architecture of the Web interface (Porter, 2008; Kostakis, 2009). Following the argument developed by Kostakis (2009), the formation of the amateur class as a class comes with the advent of the Social Web, when the amateurs start to have (more) control over the means of production and become capable of interacting (more) with each other. In the early Web, there was a surplus population eager to participate in production (Kostakis, 2009). Therefore, building heuristically on the class theory developed in Marx's work, through which one can really gain some insight into the structural reality of the Social Web, it could be argued that the reserve army of the early Web was composed of loose amateurs who had not yet formed the amateur class, as happened later in the Social Web. In the same vein, the reserve army of the Social Web still consists of some amateurs who are not advanced enough to participate in information production. This is the latent part of the working population, which consists of those who are not yet fully integrated into Social Web production. The producing amateurs, no matter their age, are regimented in platforms, either proprietary- or Commons-based, and organised in networks, while platforms are being smoothed in order to enable participation for the surplus population. With the advent of the Social Web, the exploitation of collective intelligence and creativity has been reborn, regardless of whether it is profit- and/or Commons-oriented.

Amateurs, who are at the core of proprietary-based platforms' production, remain dependent on the owners of the platforms in the same way that the owners are dependent on amateurs, who add value to the business ventures (Kostakis, 2009). This does not imply that a hacker or a professional does not use platforms, such as Facebook or Flickr, adding value to them; however, as mentioned above, it is the amateurs who came to the fore in the Social Web. The owners of the platforms can be considered as the Social Web capitalists, who renounce their dependence on the current regime of information accumulation through intellectual property and become enablers of social participation. They combine open and closed elements in the architecture of their platforms to ensure a measure of profit and control (Bauwens, 2005a, 2005b, 2007). The production of proprietary-based platforms leads, amongst others, to two types of economies: the sharing/aggregation economy and the crowdsourcing one.

In sharing/aggregation economies, for instance YouTube or Facebook, users share creative content while the owners of the platform sell their aggregated attention to advertisers (Kostakis, 2009). Moreover, platforms like Flickr make money not only from advertising, but also from the so-called Freemium model: users, who share their creations through a platform of aggregated attention, want to gain benefits from more services and pay subscription fees for getting a pro account (Anderson, 2009). But still, aggregated attention is normally a precondition for a Freemium model to work (for example, it could be assumed that subscribed users have joined the Flickr platform that includes thousands of people interested in photography, and thus the former can share and exhibit their work to a large community). Even the search engine of Google—which is not standard any more, as it depends on highly relevant advertising and thus produces very personalised results based on users' surfing behaviour (Pariser, 2011)—gains its competitive advantage from its capability to exploit the vast content created by users, as the ranking algorithm depends on the shared links towards, say, a webpage (Brin & Page, 1998). And like Flickr, Google makes money from both advertising and Freemium (it sells special services to companies). Also, with the advent of the Social Web, a torrent of user-driven pornographic sites, like YouPorn or Redtube, has been unleashed, where users share pornographic videos and photographs arising ethical issues such as that of privacy (for example, one can upload a sex video with one's ex-girlfriend or ex-boyfriend with a revenge motive) or of child pornography. These proprietary-based platforms generate profits from combining the advertising and the Freemium models. Therefore, in sharing/aggregation economies it is basically the aggregation function and/or the Freemium model that generates profits for platforms owners. However, following Pariser (2011), it should be emphasised that the shared content and users' behaviour have recently become a commodity for the owners of proprietary-based platforms, like Google or Facebook, which, in an effort to maximise the effectiveness (and thus revenues) of advertising, try to learn increasingly more about users and provide targeted, personalised advertisement: 'a perfect reflection of our interests and desires' (Pariser, 2011, p. 12). All this leads, according to Pariser (2011, p. 14), to a filter bubble and 'a world constructed from the familiar ... a world in which there is nothing to learn'.

Crowdsourcing economies are not very different to the sharing ones because there users still 'share', in a way, content, which is information. However, in crowdsourcing, the main recipient of users' input is normally the company itself. It is the shared content that contributes directly to firms' main functions and thus to profit generation. Compared with the sharing/aggregation economies, the profit motive for users here is a bit stronger, mainly in the form of a prize. Howe (2008) offers case histories such as iStockphoto, a community-driven source for stock photography, and InnoCentive, where firms offer cash prizes for solving some of their thorniest development problems. Other crowdsourcing platforms are the 99designs or the DesignCrowd, which both deal with design (from logo design to T-shirt design).

In the Web literature, one can find a myriad of different understandings and interpretations of timely concepts and buzzwords, such as sharing economy or crowdsourcing. In this paper, the first simple distinction is made on the basis of the 'workplace' of information production (proprietary- and Commons-based platforms) and then of the business model that is followed in each case (sharing/aggregation economy and crowdsourcing, which are quite relevant concepts). In essence, platform owners, who are crucially dependent on the trust of user communities, exploit in different ways the aggregated attention and the input of the networks as they enable it (Bauwens, 2007). As Bauwens (2007) points out, platforms like YouTube, Flickr or Facebook are dangerous as trustees of the common value that is created due to their speculative nature and the opaque architecture (closed source) of their platforms. The former stands for sharing/aggregation economies, because in crowdsourcing, most of the times, the rules and the processes are quite clear: users produce value for firms, and they get certain prizes or rewards in exchange (sometimes they may get nothing more than the pleasure of contribution). According to Rushkoff (2007), crowdsourcing can be understood 'as kind of industrial age, corporatist framing of a cultural phenomenon'. A company sees this phenomenon positively as 'this new affinity group population to be exploited as a resource' (Rushkoff, 2007). No common value is created, in contrast to many cases of the sharing/aggregation economy where users' input results in the creation of vast common-use value.

The Social Web exhibits both emancipatory and exploitative aspects, and the role of the users, whether they be amateurs, professionals or hackers, is to foster one over the other. It may seem that users give up some rights to the owners of the platforms to receive the chance to create, interact and satisfy their higher needs (Kostakis, 2009). On the other hand, the owners aim at maximising the aggregated attention in order to generate profit. Is this really a win–win situation, or can users do more as key agents of social change? This remains to be answered in the following sections where the sphere of the information Commons will be discussed.

Commons-based platforms

The modern history of information (or digital) Commons, i.e. socially created value that belongs to the public domain, begins with FOSS in the mid-1980s. Later, forced by the rapid development of the Internet, it is Wikipedia, Peer-to-Peer (P2P) file-sharing systems and platforms driven by voluntary communities like LibriVox that came to the fore. The Social Web is emerging, unleashing torrents of information to the public domain under Commons licences (think of the Creative Commons Licenses or the General Public Licenses): from the blogosphere to alternative media hubs such as Indymedia or even the controversial WikiLeaks, and from the Internet Archive platform to several openly accessible, peer-reviewed journals. A huge number of the aforementioned projects, such as FOSS or Wikipedia, are developed through the collaboration of dispersed communities of volunteers organised in Commons-based platforms, i.e. platforms not owned by a private entity geared towards profit maximisation, but which are owned by non-profit entities (take, for example, the Wikimedia Foundation that supports the Wikipedia project or the GNU project initiated by the Free Software Foundation). It is important to emphasise that there is a difference between profit maximisation, which may have several negative externalities to society, and profit generation, which can contribute to the sustainability of a collaborative project.

The term 'information Commons' conceptualises the deep affinities amongst all these forms of online collaboration and helps validate their distinctive social dynamics and generalise them as significant forces in economic and cultural production (Bollier, cited in Laisne *et al.*, 2010). In this study, Commons-based platforms are considered to be those 'workplaces' of information production where users consciously participate in meaningful projects, producing use value and certain products for the public domain. The incentives are mainly non-monetary (Chakravarty *et al.*, 2007; Lakhani & Wolf, 2005; Ghosh, 2005; Benkler, 2006; 2011), similar to those of the sharing/aggregation economies (i.e. reputation-building; the pleasure of communication; knowledge and experience-gaining; fun, etc.) with one main difference: volunteers share the crucial principles of a common vision and participate in certain production processes enriching the Commons sphere. In addition, they normally belong to communities with stronger ties than those, if any, of the communities of proprietary platforms (Bauwens, 2007). The processes of information production in Commons-based platforms have some certain characteristics which are embraced by the term 'peer production'.

According to Benkler (2006), peer production is a more productive system for immaterial value than the market-based or the bureaucratic-state ones. It produces social happiness as it is based on intrinsic positive motivation and synergetic cooperation (Bauwens, 2005a; Benkler, 2006). Benkler (2006) makes, amongst others, two intriguing economic observations which challenge the mainstream understanding of Standard Textbook Economics (STE). Commons-based projects serve as examples where the STE's assumption that in economic production the human being solely seeks profit maximisation is turned almost upside-down: volunteers contribute to information production projects, gaining knowledge, experience, reputation and communicating with each other, i.e. motivated by intrinsic positive incentives. This does not mean that the monetary motive is totally absent; however, it is relegated to being a peripheral concept only (Benkler, 2006; Kostakis, 2009). Many aspects of human expression, according to Benkler (2006, p. 461), 'are replete with voluntarism and actions oriented primarily toward social–psychological motivations rather than market appropriation'.

The second challenge comes against the conventional wisdom that, in Benkler's (2006, p. 463) words, 'we have only two basic free transactional forms—property-based markets and hierarchically organized firms'. Commons-based peer production can be considered the third one, and it should not be treated as an exception but rather as a widespread phenomenon, which, however, for the moment, is not counted in the economic census (Benkler, 2006). 'Worse,' as Benkler (2006, p. 463) highlights, 'we do not count them [social production processes] in our institutional design.' In STE terms, what is happening in Commons-based projects can be considered, as Bauwens (2005a) maintains, 'only in the sense that individuals are free to contribute, or take what they need, following their individual inclinations, with a [sic] invisible hand bringing it all together, but without any monetary mechanism'. Hence, in contrast to markets, i.e. the holy grail of STE, in peer production the allocation of resources is not done through a market-pricing mechanism, but hybrid modes of governance are exercised, and what is generated is not profit but use value, i.e. a Commons (Bauwens, 2005a, 2005b). In essence, bottom-up innovation, collaboration, transparency, participation, sharing, community accountability, common ownership of the results, and intrinsic positive motivation are key aspects of peer production (Kostakis, 2009, 2010, 2011a, 2011b).

Commons-based projects typically flourish in states of abundance, which is arguably a natural, inherent element of information in contrast to the conventional understanding of immaterial production. The latter, through the introduction of intellectual property (IP) in the form of strict patent and copyright law, constantly tries artificially to create scarcities in order to generate profit. IP supporters claim that it offers the necessary motives, i.e. the profit/revenue motive, for information production and innovation to occur. However, there is a vast amount of literature critical of the concept of IP (for instance, Lessig, 2004; Boldrin & Levine, 2007; Patry, 2009; Bessen & Meuer, 2009; McLeod, 2007; Burrell & Coleman, 2005), which maintains that IP is actually a government grant that leads to private monopolies, and can be extremely dangerous for social innovation, culture and society, and calls for change in institutions and laws. For example, Boldrin & Levine (2007) try to show through theory and cases that IP is unnecessary for innovation, and it damages growth, prosperity and liberty. In addition, McLeod (2007) offers an account of examples where IP laws stifle creativity, privatising many forms of expression (from human genes and public space to guitar riffs), arguing that the blind embracing of enclosure is against the human right of free speech and common resources. Echoing Lessig (2004), Benkler (2006) makes the point that if this IP amok continues, then the works, say, of Disney Inc. and Elvis Presley will never enter the public domain in the same way as Mozart or Shakespeare. Further, Patry (2009), based on economic data and socio-economic theories, contributes to modern copyright debates, shedding light on the 'violence' this monopoly control exerts on discourse, arts and innovation, arguing for a copyright law reformation that will promote innovation. Information is a non-rival good with zero marginal cost of reproduction, and as Benkler (2006) notices, the public use of information increases its value creating several positive externalities. It would be useful to mention the recent global demonstrations and campaigns in which both Commons-based foundations, such as Wikimedia and Free Software Foundation, and for-profit companies, such as Google, have been taking part against the proposed copyright legislations (namely ACTA and SOPA/ PIPA), which try to create artificial scarcities in information circulation and, thus, threaten freedom, social innovation and fundamental human rights (Free Knowledge Institute, 2012) as well as to lead, according to the Free Software Foundation (2012), to a culture of surveillance and suspicion.

The social production occurring in Commons-based platforms is facilitated by free, unconstrained and creative cooperation of communities, which lowers the legal restrictive barriers to such an exchange, inventing new institutionalised ways of sharing, such as the Creative Commons or the General Public Licenses (Kostakis, 2010). These new property forms (described by the term 'peer property' coined by Bauwens, 2005a, 2005b) allow for the social reproduction of peer projects, as they are viewed to be inherently more distributive than both state property and private exclusionary property (Bauwens, 2005a, 2005b; Lessig, 2004). In terms of property, the Commons is an idea radically different from the state one (known also as 'public property'), where the state manages a certain resource on behalf of the people, and from the private property, where a private entity excludes the common use of it (Kostakis, 2009).

The state of abundance in which the Commons-based projects flourish gives rise to new modes of governance as a result of the new productive forces of production, i.e. the combination of means of labour (information and communication technology, ICT) and human labour power (a person's ability to work; in this case mostly brain power), while new relations of productions are developed. Hence, if peer production describes the processes of information production within online, collaborative, voluntary communities which produce common value using mechanisms of self-governance, then peer governance is the way that peer production is organised. It is a bottom-up mode of participative decision-making, where decisions arise from the free engagement and cooperation of producers (Bauwens, 2005a, 2005b). Coffin (2006) mentions some obvious characteristics of successful open-source/peer communities. First, membership is open and widespread, premised on participation. The free collaboration among the members is geographically dispersed, asynchronous and organised in networks. Moreover, projects are transparent, and dialogues among participants are normally recorded, with the materials of projects like Wikipedia subject to open review (often, there are mechanisms for institutional history). Therefore, at first glance, openness, networking, participation and transparency appear as the main characteristics of governance in peer projects (Kostakis, 2010). More closely, these projects do not operate in strict hierarchies of command and control, but rather in heterarchies (Bruns, 2008; Kostakis, 2010). They operate 'in a much looser [environment] which ... allows for the existence of multiple teams of participants working simultaneously in a variety of possibly opposing directions' (Bruns, 2008, p. 26). Heterachies, following Stephenson (2009), bring together elements of networks and hierarchies and are the most relevant organisational structure for peer projects, as they provide horizontal links, which allow for various elements of an organisation to collaborate, while optimising individually several success criteria. According to Bruns (2008), they are not simply adhocracies, but ad-hoc meritocracies which, however, are at risk of transforming themselves into more inflexible, strict hierarchies. In addition, following Bauwens (2005a, 2005b), peer projects are based on the organising principle of equipotentiality, i.e. everyone can potentially cooperate in a project—no authority can prejudge the ability to cooperate. In peer projects, equipotential participants self-select themselves to the section to which they want to contribute (Bauwens, 2005b).

Further, Stadler (2008) submits that leadership in most Commons-based projects is not egalitarian, but meritocratic:

> Everyone is free, indeed, to propose a contribution, but the people who run the project are equally free to reject the contribution outright. ... The core task of managing a Commons is to ensure not just the production of resources, but also to prevent its degradation from the addition of low quality material.

Moreover, benevolent dictatorships are common (Raymond, 2001; Malcolm, 2008). It can be stated that this concept actually highlights the tensions between hierarchy and equality as well as authority and autonomy in such projects. For instance, benevolent dictatorships can be found in the Linux project, where Linus Torvalds is the benevolent dictator (Malcolm, 2008), or in Wikipedia, where Jimmy Wales holds that role. Coffin (2006) highlights the necessity of a benevolent dictator (who typically is one of the founders of the project), adding that the foundation developers and the early adopters set the project ethos as well. The founder, along with the first members, exercise his/her authority over participants' contributions (for example, Torvalds decides which code will become part of the official release of the Linux project) and/or upholds the right to fork. Bruns defines benevolent dictators 'as ones of several heterarchical leaders of the community, who have risen to their positions through consistent constructive contribution and stand and fall with the quality of their further performance' (interview, cited in Kostakis, 2010). It is obvious that through such leadership roles, these benevolent dictators may need to push through unpopular decisions. As Bruns notes, 'if they abuse that power, theirs becomes a malicious leadership', and what we should expect at this point is 'a substantial exodus of community members' (interview, cited in Kostakis, 2010). Therefore, following Bruns' narrative, 'the continued existence of the project at that moment would depend very much on whether the number of exiting members can be made up for in both quality and quantity by incoming new participants' (interview, cited in Kostakis, 2010). An oft-cited depiction of the governance processes followed in peer projects, especially in FOSS, is offered by the so-called onion model (Nakakoji et al., 2002; Ye & Kishida, 2003). At the heart of the onion is sometimes a single person, the project leader, most of the times the initiator of the project. Also at the centre, supporting the project leader, there are the core members who have more authority than other project developers, having been involved for a long time with serious contribution work (that is why meritocracy is a substantial characteristic of peer governance). Beyond this, there are other roles for contributors varying on the degree of their involvement (say active developers, peripheral developers and bug fixers).

Kostakis (2010) studies the governance mechanisms of Wikipedia in order to obtain a better understanding of the structural relationships of Commons-based information production. It is true that some of Wikipedia's governance processes differ from those of FOSS projects, LibriVox and other content Commons. However, examining the shared affinities amongst such projects, the Wikipedia case served as a good chance to shed light on the basic aspects of governance and management in peer projects. The main conclusions drawn were that peer governance is actually an unfinished artefact that follows the constant reform and refinement of social forms within the community. It is a suitable mode to govern large sources, working more effectively in abundance; whereas in the scarcity realm, democratic—in the form of representation—or market-based modes tend to prevail. However, echoing O'Neil (2009), especially in large-scales projects, open participation with an increasing number of participants makes the governance of the project much more complex. Examining the internal battle between inclusionists and deletionists, it was understood that Wikipedia's lack of a clearly defined constitution bred a danger for local jurisdictions where small numbers of participants create rules in conflict with others (O'Neil, 2009). These challenge the sustainability of the peer project. During conflicts, persistent, well-organised minorities can adroitly handle and dominate their opponents. The values of communal evaluation and equipotentiality are subverted by such practices. As Hilbert (2007, p. 120) remarks, group polarisation is a significant danger that open, online communities face: 'Discourse among like-minded people can very quickly lead to group polarization ... which causes opinions to diverge rather than converge ... [so], it is very probable that the strongest groups will dominate the common life.' In these cases, transparency and holoptism are in danger. Decisions are being made in secret, and power is being accumulated. Authority, corruption, hidden hierarchies and secrecy subvert the foundations of peer governance, which are openness, heterarchy, transparency, equipotentiality and holoptism. Moreover, Freeman (1970) argues that in seemingly structure-less groups, hidden structures may impose different things on the rest; this is described as 'the tyranny of the structurelessness'.

Especially when abundance is replaced by scarcity (as happened in Wikipedia when deletionists demanded a strict content control), power structures emerge as peer-governance mechanisms cannot function well (Kostakis, 2010). Hoeschele (2010, pp. 19–20) suggests that there are three ways that scarcity, i.e. 'the condition when available goods do not meet demands', can be generated:

> First, the total amount of a good or service can be reduced. For example, the expansion of market activities may reduce the amount of goods provided by nature (such as clean air). ... Second, barriers can be placed between people and a good. Of potentially many ways to obtain that good, only one or a few may be left available, leading to the creation of a bottleneck. ... Third, new wants or needs can be created, or existing ones modified, so that demand for a commodity exceeds supply. ... All three basic mechanisms not only increase scarcity, but also curtail freedom by forcing increased expenditures on people and reducing available options of how to satisfy their needs.

'Throughout history,' Hoeschele maintains, 'we can conceive of social power as having been based in part on the construction of scarcity.' That is why abundance is a key to Commons-based projects' sustainability (Kostakis, 2011b). Peer production reintroduces, and is based on, the importance of abundance, making evident that social imagination and creativity become unpredictable, since an abundant intellect (i.e. the surplus creativity of people) can have access to resources (information), tools (ICT) and goods (information as final product) (Kostakis, 2011b).

Furthermore, the reintroduction of certain elements of traditional organisation (hierarchy or market) contributes to their sustainability as well (Loubser & den Basten, 2008; Benkler, 2006), whenever there is a need to manage scarcity. A benevolent dictatorship can be the result of spontaneous hierarchy that emerges when important decisions for the project are to be taken, in which the leader/founder, whose sole role is to serve the community, has authority which comes from responsibility and not from the power to coerce (Raymond, 2001; Weber, 2004). These elements are, after all, part of what is understood as peer governance—a heterarchical, hybrid mode of organisation which combines traditional modes of organisation with networked-based ones (Kostakis, 2009, 2011b); or, to quote Weber (2004, p. 189), 'an imperfect mix of leadership, informal coordination mechanisms, implicit and explicit norms, along with some formal governance structures that are evolving and doing so at a rate that has been sufficient to hold surprisingly complex systems together'.

Instead of conclusions: chances for reflection on our institutional design

Light has been shed on the structural relationships of information production with a focus on certain essential concepts for political economy, i.e. labour, property and governance. In proprietary-based platforms, it might seem that there is a win–win model with profit generation for the owners and satisfaction of users' higher needs such as communication, reputation-building and knowledge gain. The owners of the platforms renounce their dependence on the regime of artificial scarcity, celebrating an age of information abundance while enabling social participation. However, as mentioned, the architecture of proprietary platforms combines open and closed elements to ensure a measure of profit and control. This makes proprietary platforms dangerous as trustees of the common use value. Moreover, issues and problems such as privacy and electronic surveillance; exploitation; and online manipulation and control, come to the fore due to owners' speculative nature. Hence, the Internet and its Social Web platforms exhibit both emancipatory and exploitative aspects, and the political struggle of online communities and users should be to foster the one over the other, strengthening the Commons sphere. The Commons-based peer production brings to the fore, amongst others, two ideas which have been consistently neglected in the design processes of the modern institutional systems of Western societies. Firstly, it is the power of human cooperation that becomes evident through the study of the social production which is taking place on the Web. As Benkler (2011) elaborates, the currently dominant socio-economic paradigm is premised on the idea that humans are driven solely by self-interest, guided by the invisible hand of the market or the iron fist of a centralised government. Benkler draws conclusions from hundreds of diverse studies and uses a large amount of case studies, amongst others many Commons-based peer production projects, to show 'how cooperation trumps self-interest—maybe not all the time, for everyone, but far more consistently than we've long thought' (p. 249). We, as a society, following Benkler's thought, should dedicate 'the next fifty years to the vastly more complex but infinitely more rewarding task of designing the systems we inhabit for the kind of diverse, complex, but overall fair-minded, moral, sociable, and humane beings we in fact are' (p. 249). Furthermore, it was claimed that the concept of abundance, in relation to the emergence of power structures and autonomy, is another idea that the social production of the Web has brought to the forefront. It was argued how abundance resists to the emergence of power structures in the online communities of peer projects, giving rise to new modes of governance, i.e. peer governance. It can be also articulated that in the social production of the Web abundance and autonomy seem interrelated concepts: information, inherently abundant with zero-marginal costs, and the cheap ICT, i.e. both essential means of production, are distributed to the people who are eager to contribute to the creation, the advancement and the enrichment of the Commons sphere. Thus, it can be claimed that the productive models, premised on abundance and, thus, autonomy, exemplified by FOSS or Wikipedia, should be counted in the institutional designs in the fore-coming years; wherever it is possible, we should pull down the barriers of artificial scarcity, often set by legal restrictive regimes, enabling abundance. If nanotechnology and engineering succeed in making capabilities such as desktop manufacturing and three-dimensional (3D) printing—a technology which has the potential to transcend mass production, being more flexible, productive, customisable and cost-effective (*The Economist*, 2011a, 2011b, 2011c)—accessible to the masses by dropping the costs (in the fashion of microprocessors evolution since the 1970s), the possibilities for the current information-based techno-economic paradigm become arguably unprecedented, connecting the social production on the Web with the low marginal costs of material production and the do-it-yourself (DIY) culture (for an informative account of DIY and open design movements, see van Abel *et al.*, 2011). Think of collaboratively designing a car, like software, and be able to produce its parts using desktop manufacturing technologies and setting them up, say, like IKEA furniture. Then, what may lie ahead might be, to put it in the Perezian style (Perez, 2002), a 'Golden Age', in terms of innovation, prosperity, development and well-being, built upon creative synergies and alliances amongst Commons-based communities, the market and the state.

Acknowledgements

The author would like to express his gratitude to Wolfgang Drechsler, Carlota Perez, Michel Bauwens and Axel Bruns, as well as to the anonymous referees for their useful comments. The research was supported by the Grant Numbers SF 014006, 'Challenges to State Modernization in 21st Century Europe', and ETF 8571, 'Web 2.0 and Governance: Institutional and Normative Changes and Challenges'.

References

Anderson, C. (2009) *Free: the future of a radical price* (New York, NY, Hyperion).
Bauwens, M. (2005a) The political economy of peer production, *Ctheory Journal*. Available online at: http://www.ctheory.net/articles.aspx?id=499 (accessed 25 February 2012).
Bauwens, M. (2005b) Peer to peer and human evolution, *Integral Visioning*. Available online at: http://integralvisioning.org/article.php?story=p2ptheory1 (accessed 25 February 2012).
Bauwens, M. (2007) The Social Web and its social contracts: some notes on social antagonism in netarchical capitalism, *Re-public*, Available online at: http://www.re-public.gr/en/?p=261 (accessed 25 February 2012).
Benkler, Y. (2006) *The wealth of networks: how social production transforms markets and freedom* (New Haven, CT, and London, Yale University Press).
Benkler, Y. (2011) *The penguin and the leviathan* (New York, NY, Crown Business).
Bessen, J. & Meuer, M. (2009) *How judges, bureaucrats, and lawyers put innovators at risk* (Princeton, NJ, Princeton University Press).
Boldrin, M. & Levine, D. (2007) *Against intellectual monopoly* (New York, NY, Cambridge University Press).
Brin, S. & Page, L. (1998) The anatomy of a large-scale hypertextual web search engine, paper presented at the *7th International World-Wide-Web Conference*, Brisbane, QLD, Australia, April, 14–18, 1998.
Bruns, A. (2008) *Blogs, Wikipedia, Second Life, and beyond: from production to produsage* (New York, NY, Peter Lang).
Burrell, R. & Coleman, A. (2005) *The digital impact* (Cambridge, Cambridge University Press).
Chakravarty, S., Haruvy, E. & Wu, F. (2007) The link between incentives and product performance in open source development: an empirical investigation, *Global Business and Economics Review*, 9, 151–169.
Coffin, J. (2006) Analysis of open source principles in diverse collaborative communities, *First Monday*, 11(6). Available online at: http://firstmonday.org/htbin/cgiwrap/bin/ojs/index.php/fm/article/view/1342/1262 (accessed 25 February 2012).
Free Knowledge Institute (2012) *ACTA: a global threat to freedom (open letter)*. Available online at: http://freeknowledge.eu/acta-a-global-threat-to-freedoms-open-letter (accessed 25 February 2012).
Free Software Foundation (2012) *Speak out against ACTA*. Available online at: http://freeknowledge.eu/acta-a-global-threat-to-freedoms-open-letter (accessed 25 February 2012).
Freeman, J. (1970) The tyranny of structurelessness, *Berkeley Journal of Sociology*, 17, 151–165.
Ghosh, R. (2005) Understanding free software developers: findings from the FLOSS Study, in: J. Feller, B. Fitzgerald, S. Hissam & K. Lakhani (Eds) *Perspectives on free and open source software* (Cambridge, MA, MIT Press).
Hilbert, M. (2007) *Digital processes and democratic theory*. Available online at: http://www.martinhilbert.net/democracy.html (accessed 25 February 2012).
Hoeschele, W. (2010) *The economics of abundance: a political economy of freedom, equity, and sustainability* (Aldershot, Gower).
Howe, J. (2006) The rise of crowdsourcing, *Wired*. Available online at: http://www.wired.com/wired/archive/14.06/crowds.html (accessed 25 February 2012).
Howe, J. (2008) *Crowdsourcing: why the power of the crowd is driving the future of business* (New York, NY, Crown Business).
Kleiner, D. & Wyrick, B. (2007) InfoEnclosure 2.0, *Mute*. Available online at: http://www.metamute.org/en/InfoEnclosure-2.0 (accessed 25 February 2012).
Kostakis, V. (2009) The amateur class, or, the reserve army of the Web, *Rethinking Marxism*, 21(3), 457–461.
Kostakis, V. (2010) Identifying and understanding the problems of Wikipedia's peer governance, *First Monday*, 15(3), Available online at: http://firstmonday.org/htbin/cgiwrap/bin/ojs/index.php/fm/article/view/2613/2479 (accessed 25 February 2012).
Kostakis, V. (2011a) The advent of open source democracy and wikipolitics: challenges, threats and opportunities for democratic discourse, *Human Technology*, 7(1), 9–29.

Kostakis, V. (2011b) Commons-based peer production and the neo-Weberian state: synergies and interdependencies, *Halduskultuur—Administrative Culture*, 12(2), 146–161.

Laisne, J., Aigrain, P., Bollier, D. & Tiemann, M. (2010) *2020 FLOSS roadmap* (3rd edn). Available online at: http://www.2020flossroadmap.org (accessed 25 February 2012).

Lakhani, K. & Wolf, R. (2005) Why hackers do what they do: understanding motivation and effort in free/open source software projects, in: J. Feller, B. Fitzgerald, S. Hissam & K. Lakhani (Eds) *Perspectives on free and open source software* (Cambridge, MA, MIT Press), 3–22.

Lessig, L. (2004) *Free culture* (New York, NY, Penguin).

Levy, S. (2001) *Hackers: heroes of the computer revolution* (New York, NY, Penguin).

Loubser, M. & den Besten, M. (2008) *Wikipedia admins and templates: the organizational capabilities of a peer production effort*, Available online at: http://papers.ssrn.com/sol3/papers.cfm?abstract_id=1116171 (accessed 25 February 2012).

Malcolm, J. (2008) *Multi-stakeholder governance and the Internet Governance Forum* (Perth, Terminus).

Marx, K. (1992) *Capital*, Vol. 1: *A critique of political economy* (London, Penguin) (Original work published 1867).

Marx, K. (1993) *Grundrisse: foundations of the critique of political economy (rough draft)* (London, Penguin); orig. *Grundrisse der Kritik der Politischen Ökonomie (Rohentwurf) 1858*. Marx-Engels-Werke (MEW) 42 (Berlin, Dietz 1983).

McLeod, K. (2007) *Freedom of expression* (Minneapolis, MI, University of Minnesota Press).

Nakakoji, K., Yamamoto, Y., Nishinaka, Y., Kishida, K. & Yunwen, Y. (2002) Evolution patterns of open-source software systems and communities, *Proceedings of International Workshop on Principles of Software Evolution*, Available online at: http://www.kid.rcast.u-tokyo.ac.jp/~kumiyo/mypapers/IWPSE2002.pdf (accessed 25 February 2012).

O'Neil, M. (2009) *Cyberchiefs: autonomy and authority in online tribes* (London, Pluto).

O'Reilly, T. (2006) Web 2.0 compact definition: trying again, *O'Reilly Radar*. Available online at: http://radar.oreilly.com/2006/12/web-20-compact-definition-tryi.html (accessed 25 February 2012).

Pariser, E. (2011) *The filter bubble* (New York, NY, Penguin Viking).

Patry, W. (2009) *Moral panics and the copyright war* (New York, NY, Oxford University Press).

Perez, C. (2002) *Technological revolutions and financial capital: the dynamics of bubbles and golden ages* (Cheltenham, Edward Elgar).

Porter, J. (2008) *Designing for the Social Web* (Berkeley, CA, New Riders).

Raymond, E. (2001) *The cathedral and the bazaar* (Sebastopol, CA, O'Reilly Media).

Rushkoff, D. (2007) What does crowdsourcing really mean? *Wired*. Available online at: http://www.wired.com/techbiz/media/news/2007/07/crowdsourcing?currentPage=1 (accessed 25 February 2012).

Stadler, F. (2008) *On the differences between open source and open culture*. Available online at: http://publication.nodel.org/On-the-Differences (accessed 25 February 2012).

Stephenson, K. (2009) Neither hierarchy nor network: an argument for heterarchy, *People and Strategy*, 32(1), 4–13.

The Economist (2011a) The printed world, *Economist Online*. Available online at: http://www.economist.com/node/18114221 (accessed 25 February 2012).

The Economist (2011b) Difference Engine: making it, *Economist Online*. Available online at: http://www.economist.com/blogs/babbage/2011/11/3d-printing (accessed 25 February 2012).

The Economist (2011c) The shape of things to come. *Economist Online*. Available online at: http://www.economist.com/node/21541382 (accessed 25 February 2012).

Van Abel, B., Evers, L., Klaassen, R. & Troxler, P. (2011) *Open design now* (Amsterdam, BIS).

Wark, M. (2004) *A hacker manifesto* (Cambridge, MA, Harvard University Press).

Weber, S. (2004) *The success of open source* (Cambridge, MA, Harvard University Press).

Ye, Y. & Kishida, K. (2003) Toward an understanding of the motivation of open source software developers, *Proceedings of the 25th International Conference on Software Engineering* (San Diego, CA, ACM Press), 419–429.

Social intermediaries and the location of agency: a conceptual reconfiguration of social network sites

Martin Berg

Halmstad University, School of Social and Health Sciences, Halmstad, Sweden

Over recent years significant changes in the nature of online communication have taken place, not the least because of the emergence of Web 2.0 and the subsequent proliferation of Social Network Sites (SNS). These changes illuminate the need for having a precise conceptual apparatus that can grasp the complexity of contemporary online phenomena and their social dynamics. Exploring various accounts of SNS as part of the wider Web 2.0 realm, this paper approaches the widespread assumption that SNS bring forth a number of changes in the social as well as institutional arrangements surrounding their being used. Distinguishing between an instrumental and an institutional approach towards SNS, this paper suggests that contemporary research on SNS is roughly divided into two broad streams, one that focuses on how SNS are brought into service by users, and the other on how SNS bring users into service. The difference between these approaches is framed by suggesting a conceptual separation between individual-oriented and system-oriented agency. In order to overcome the difficulties attached to understanding the social dynamics of SNS as a distinct application within the Web 2.0 realm, it is argued that the term 'social intermediaries' offers a way to conceptualise SNS with respect to their functional position in the social realm, thus providing an important alternative to contemporary instrumental and institutional accounts.

Introduction

Over recent years significant changes in the nature of online communication have taken place, not the least because of the emergence of Web 2.0 and the subsequent proliferation of what boyd and Ellison (2007) have termed Social Network Sites (SNS). These changes have provided researchers, scholars and critics with a multi-levelled field of investigation, while at the same time illuminating the need for having a precise conceptual apparatus that can grasp the complexity of contemporary online phenomena and their social dynamics. Exploring various accounts of SNS as part of the wider Web 2.0 realm, this paper approaches the widespread assumption that SNS bring forth a number of changes in the social as well as institutional arrangements surrounding their being used. Web 2.0 is often regarded as a 'cluster of technologies, devices, and applications that support the proliferation of social spaces in the Internet' (Castells, 2009, p. 65). These social spaces are often assumed to facilitate activities such as sharing, sorting and categorising data that is reviewed and commented upon. Even though this instrumental view of Web 2.0 is prevailing, it is possible to discern a parallel track in contemporary research that positions individual instrumentality as inferior to issues of power and institutional exploitation. Whereas the instrumental view primarily locates agency at the level of individual users and the personal benefits associated with the performance of various technologically mediated actions, the institutional view ascribes agency to the Web 2.0 applications which are assumed to commercially deploy their users as objects of inquiry and sources of information. The main difference between these approaches is that agency is located on different levels, and for this reason, a conceptual separation between individual-oriented and system-oriented agency is suggested. In this context, individual-oriented agency points at how attention is paid to how users can bring SNS into service, whereas system-oriented agency is a question of how SNS benefit from the users. Importantly, neither of these perspectives, nor the established conceptual framework, can account for the social dynamics of SNS as a distinct application within the Web 2.0 realm. In order to overcome these difficulties, it is hence argued that the term 'social intermediaries' offers a way to conceptualise SNS with respect to their functional position in the social realm, thus providing an important alternative to contemporary instrumental and institutional accounts.[1]

Egocentric networks and individual-oriented agency

A vast majority of contemporary accounts of Web 2.0 applications depart from descriptions of the presumed functionality of front-end features as well as analyses of how traditional broadcast models are challenged in a continuously changing media landscape.[2] Assuming that the media landscape of today offers vastly changed conditions for communication, it is frequently argued that Web 2.0 applications allow for an increased level of interactivity while at the same time facilitating a creative as well as collaborative processing of user-generated content of various kinds (see for instance Jenkins, 2008; Shirky, 2009, 2010; Gauntlett, 2011). An illuminating example of this latter perception is provided by Beer and Burrows who suggest that Web 2.0 can be regarded as 'dynamic matrices of information through which people observe others, expand the network, make new "friends", edit and update content, blog, remix, post, respond, share files, exhibit, tag and so on' (2007, para. 2.1). Taking this definition into consideration, it is apparent that the umbrella concept Web 2.0 cannot fully account for the vast array of features to which it refers. Elaborating on this idea, Beer (2008) underscores that one of the key problems facing researchers when trying to make sense of contemporary online cultures is the plethora of definitions and concepts that tend to be inconsistent and characterised by a certain fluidity. In the context of Web 2.0 applications, the difficulties attached to defining their general characteristics become especially apparent in the case of SNS. It is widely claimed that SNS allow for the creation of a public or semi-public profile which facilitates various form of connectivity. With such a unidirectional focus on how the performance of various tasks is facilitated by SNS, many researchers tend to presume an individual-centred agency, thus ignoring, or perhaps defusing the importance of database actions and structuring mechanisms. Approaching the social significance of SNS by focusing on individual concerns and front-end features, it is hard to account for the conditions under which SNS are utilised. Furthermore, such an approach easily fails to elucidate how SNS are part and parcel of new media business models and their attempts to manipulate and predict online interaction (Andrejevic, 2011).

Situating the use of SNS as deeply embedded in everyday life, current research on the social significance of these sites often strikes a balance between online and offline modes of social interaction. In line with such an understanding, it has been demonstrated that SNS are mainly used to maintain and sustain offline relationships (Lampe *et al.*, 2006; Ellison *et al.*, 2007). Similarly, it has been shown that online and offline networks supplement, rather than replace each other, and thus as boyd (2008) suggests, provide their users with a 'networked public' that supports social interaction in a fashion similar to offline contexts (see also McKenna *et al.*, 2002; Valenzuela *et al.*, 2009; Vergeer & Pelzer, 2009). Although these observations are important for the study of SNS, a singular focus on how SNS are instrumentally deployed in everyday life runs the risk of supporting an understanding of these phenomena as user-driven and thus also unproblematic. Without explicitly recognising that most SNS are commercial products and thus deeply embedded in the mechanisms of contemporary capitalist society, boyd and Ellison (2007) support such an understanding when maintaining that the emergence of SNS marks a fundamental shift in the history of online interaction. Arguing that this shift involves a move from thematically organised online communities to 'egocentric' networks revolving around individuals, the authors fail to notice that SNS also involve the emergence of a certain kind of mechanisms that codify, constrain and regulate social interaction. To take but one example, Facebook allows for the sharing of certain kinds of information in a limited number of forms, and by default displays only selected information to users. The latter feature is mainly driven by the algorithm 'EdgeRank' that has been described as 'the secret sauce that makes Facebook's News Feed tick' (Kincaid, 2010). Instead of illuminating these aspects of SNS, researchers are frequently inclined to focus mainly on the concerns and practices of individual users, which is exemplified by the recent interest in Toffler's (1980) term 'prosumer' along with Bruns' (2008) term 'produser' that both refer to processes of technological and cultural change while placing the individual at the centre of attention (see also Beer & Burrows, 2010; Ritzer & Jurgenson, 2010; Bird, 2011).

A particularly important example of how research on SNS fails to account for more than front-end matters is found in the ways in which personal integrity and privacy concerns have been discussed. Recent investigations into the nature of SNS frequently return to problems related to how personal information is handled and secured. Although studies have demonstrated that the public nature of SNS remains unclear to many users (Stutzman, 2006) and that there is a fundamental discrepancy between users' desire for privacy protection and their actual behaviour (Acquisti & Gross, 2006), questions of privacy and integrity are most often discussed without taking back-end processes of monitoring into account (Andrejevic, 2011). Rather, these matters have been treated by paying attention to complicated privacy settings and the difficulties associated with upholding personal integrity online (see also Dwyer *et al.*, 2007; Debatin *et al.*, 2009).

Although illuminating important characteristics of SNS, research that mainly considers front-end characteristics and dimensions of personal utility forecloses any possibility to critically analyse the institutional facets of these phenomena. Understanding SNS as providing the infrastructural basis for users to pursue their personal interests and goals, the question of how the presumed interactivity is intertwined with the social situation in which it occurs (as suggested by Mead, 1934; Giddens, 1991; Simmel, 2009/1908 among others) is left out of consideration. On this note, Jarrett (2008) underscores that the term interactivity presumes an already existent agency which is necessarily rooted in the social mechanisms of Web 2.0 applications such as SNS. Arguing against more cheerful interpretations of SNS that seem to understand these applications and sites as disembedded from the social and political reality of which they are part, Jarrett makes clear that their singularly most important function is to provide users with the means to engage in social interaction and various forms of informational production. Although SNS are often claimed to facilitate the articulation of individual and social action, Jarrett emphasises that such a change in agency goes hand in hand with the social environment in which it occurs. This means that SNS do not so much allow for a high level of interactivity as for the creation of a desire and capacity to interact. Any attempt to grasp these matters thus needs to take a critical stance towards the idea that SNS promote an increased level of interactivity while also providing a playground for the production and consumption of user-generated content. In so doing, as Jarrett suggests, the notion of interactivity would be found to offer a 'contingent freedom, complete with an effective set of chains binding people to the neoliberal hegemony' (2008, para. 33). Similarly, Allen (2008) maintains that the broader realm of Web 2.0 needs to be understood as a multimodal phenomenon that not only involves design and basic functionality but also certain business models aiming at putting 'people and data together in meaningful exchanges' (2008, para. 7). Following this line of thought, Allen suggests that we are dealing with services that bring a new kind of media consumer into being as a result of the constant encouragement to create, maintain and expand various forms of content.

In the above discussion, it has been argued that many accounts of SNS direct their attention to front-end characteristics while focusing on the presumed concerns of users. While these matters are important to consider, it would be a mistake not to expand the scope of analysis beyond the visible surface of these sites. Importantly, SNS amount to both a communicative means and the very boundaries of the online social situation. This state of affairs suggests that Web 2.0 in general and SNS in particular undeniably need to be conceptualised by taking into account a wider array of issues than the ones presented above. Front-end characteristics are fundamentally important for the experience of using SNS but in order to account for the social dynamics of these social spaces, it is decisive not to assume that users enter the communicative situation as agential subjects unencumbered by the constraints of those very spaces. Such an understanding, however, is most often promoted within this stream of research since it fails to acknowledge that front-end characteristics are largely the result of complex back-end structures, algorithms and processes.

Labour under siege and system-oriented agency

The widespread approach towards SNS from the perspective of front-end matters and individual concerns has not been left without substantial criticism. Instead of focusing on the visible surface of these sites and on how they are put into use, a number of researchers have turned their attention to back-end mechanisms in order to account for how users are exploited for the purpose of revenue (see for instance Fuchs, 2008, 2010 for a general account of these matters). Gehl provides an illuminating example of this approach when putting forward a definition of Web 2.0 that seems to be a world apart from the instrumentally oriented interpretations that were outlined above. Focusing mainly on back-end features and overall socio-economic circumstances, he argues that the realm of Web 2.0 applications should be understood as 'the new media capitalist technique of relying upon users to supply and rank online media content, then using the attention this content generates to present advertisements to audiences' (2011, p. 2). This argument involves an analytical leap, from front-end characteristics into back-end mechanisms, while simultaneously situating both as deeply embedded in macroscopical processes that characterise late modernity. These matters are particularly visible in the case of SNS since their framing of user activities, to a larger extent than other Web 2.0 applications, depend upon back-end mechanisms.

Paying close attention to back-end processes and mechanisms as well as the economic forces in which these are embedded, Gehl points at the insufficiency of simply illuminating the various kinds of actions and interactions in which users engage. Rather, he maintains that these sites forcefully encourage users to focus solely on the interface through which '[t]hey are expected to process digital objects by sharing content, making connections, ranking cultural artifacts, and producing digital content' (2011, p. 2). Along with Andrejevic (2011) among others, Gehl calls for an analysis of hegemony rather than intentionality in the wider context of Web 2.0 applications. A similar idea is put forward by Zimmer (2008b, para. 2), who suggests that there is a certain rhetoric suggesting 'that everyone can and should use new Internet technologies to organise and share information, to interact within communities, and to express oneself' (see also Beer & Burrows, 2007).

Although the course of history of internet studies is permeated with an expectation and desire for technologically supported social spaces to facilitate creative empowerment and democratisation (see for instance Rheingold, 1995; Turkle, 1995; Benedikt, 2000/1991), we are now dealing with a certain kind of mechanisms that affect the ways in which online social interaction is formed. Importantly, these mechanisms are part of certain business models that rely on the continuous exploitation of free labour, and necessarily need to be ascribed with a certain amount of agency. The extensive commercialisation of SNS has led to the creation of algorithms and mechanisms that encourage users to interact (i.e. provide data) and this means that 'the desires of users did not grow in a vacuum; they are largely created by the market machine in the first place' (Scholz, 2008, para. 2). Following Scholtz's argument, it is clear that SNS cannot be solely conceptualised as social spaces in which 'prosumers' engage in collaborative practices of sharing, sorting and categorising data. Rather, there is an obvious need to consider how these practices partially result from and are motivated by external structures and processes.

The widespread interest in front-end features, against which researchers such as Gehl, Zimmer and Scholz among others react, can to some amount be traced back to the point where O'Reilly coined the term Web 2.0. Until that day, the worldwide web had largely been characterised by static content and one-way directed publishing systems. In contrast, Web 2.0 was associated with a completely different architecture that allowed for participation and collaboration. It was not until some years later that O'Reilly publicly maintained that 'Web 2.0 was a pretty crappy name for what's happening /.../ [It] is not about front-end technologies. It's precisely about back-end, and it's about meaning and intelligence in the back-end' (quoted in Scholz, 2008).[3] Taking his words seriously, it seems plausible to suggest that many efforts to interpret the wider realm of Web 2.0 applications have been caught in a loop of continuously returning to the visually graspable, thus rendering back-end mechanisms and operations unimportant. Instead of questioning the underlying structures of this kind of online spaces, researchers have highlighted various aspects of participatory culture, the creative potential of user-generated content, and thereby positioning the 'prosumer' as a specific personage of the digital age. Although SNS and other kinds of applications within the Web 2.0 realm undeniably allow for a certain creativity and to some extent personal autonomy, it is decisive not forget that these sites and applications are 'always entrenched in market relationships, no matter if users are motivated by profit' (Scholz, 2008, para. 38). As have been made clear earlier, these matters are frequently overlooked, and this state of affairs makes it increasingly complicated to understand the externalities of Web 2.0 applications (Zimmer, 2008a).

In order to establish a fair understanding of SNS, it is important to separate the actual meaning of these sites from commercial attempts to, as Silver puts it, 'conflate community and commerce, citizen and consumer' (2008, para. 8). Such an approach necessarily needs to take into account that we are dealing with phenomena that are deeply embedded in a discursive formation chiefly emanating from corporate actors. Taking a critical stance toward corporate hegemony, that obviously prefer profits in favour of public goods, is an important part of deconstructing the contradictory relationship between front-end features and back-end mechanisms. As Gehl argues, 'the smooth interfaces that users enjoy appear to be comprised solely of immediate connections and instant information' (2011, p. 2), but it is decisive to have in mind that these interfaces are but the tip of an iceberg. Continuing his argument, Gehl underscores that we are not simply dealing with 'spaces where users take control of content creation /.../ they are also devices designed to capture the affective labor of users and create archives of the digital material they produce' (2011, p. 3). Building upon aggregated data, profiling, surveillance, sorting and data mining, these archives construct virtual data-doubles of user activity in which selves are 'broken up into a series of data flows' (McStay, 2011, p. 311) based on traces and signifiers. It is thus important to have in mind that all kinds of social interaction on SNS 'become data points in algorithms for sorting, predicting, and managing our behaviour' (Andrejevic 2011, p. 287).

The corporate monitoring, storing and processing of data clearly involve a set of asymmetrical power relations through which 'the subjects of communication become objects of information' (Fuchs, 2011, p. 304). In effect, SNS and the wider realm of Web 2.0 applications are supported by an infrastructure that on the one hand fosters interaction, participation and creativity, but on the other hand 'enables companies easily to piggyback on user generated content' (Petersen, 2008, para. 1). Alluding the words of O'Reilly, Petersen elaborates this idea further and suggests that 'the architecture of participation sometimes turns into an architecture of exploitation' (2008, para. 1). Pointing at the necessity of acknowledging that the broader category of Web 2.0 phenomena is always deeply embedded in capitalist structures (see also Terranova, 2004), Petersen argues that '[i]t is when the technological infrastructure and design of these sites is combined with capitalism that the architecture begins to oscillate between exploitation and participation' (2008, para. 24). In a similar vein, Beer and Burrows (2007) underscore the importance of situating these phenomena in the context of what Thrift (2005) has termed 'knowing capitalism'. Thrift argues that software and social processes have become increasingly interwoven and that software affects everyday life from a background position. These changes do not only provide an 'automatic production of space which has important consequences for what we regard as the world's phenomenality' (Thrift, 2005, p. 153) but also challenge the very notion of how space is animated (see also Dean, 2010). Following this line of thought, Beer and Burrows point at the importance of recognising SNS as commercial spaces since they routinely harvest information about users, thus pointing at a problematic aspect of their being free to use. Even though these accounts more or less declare Web 2.0 as a cluster of informational machines that routinely exploit users, thus creating desires and sometimes fear, it is important to note that these processes do not take place without the active participation of users. In this respect, this stream of research appears to neglect the fundamental insights of the perspective that favours an individual-oriented agency thus being incapable of grasping the meanings that are attached to SNS by users.

Towards a reconfigured conceptual apparatus

From the preceding exploration it is clear that there are discrepancies in how the wider domain of Web 2.0 applications is approached and conceptualised. These differences are mainly due to where agency is located, and consequently how either front-end features or back-end mechanisms are emphasised. While the perspective that assumes an individual-oriented agency stresses the importance of front-end features and the presumed utility value of various applications and sites, little attention is paid to what is going on back-end. In contrast, the perspective that assumes a system-oriented agency challenges such an account of Web 2.0 applications by putting back-end features in the centre of attention and thereby highlighting the institutional characteristics of these phenomena. Although these perspectives occasionally converge, it is noticeable that their particular concerns are kept at a distance from each other since no satisfactory connection is established between the questions of how users can bring SNS into service and how SNS benefit from user activity. Elaborating this observation further, these differences are possible to perceive of as related to various degrees of structural sensitivity since the former perspective is rather reluctant to acknowledge the structural conditioning of interactions mediated by SNS, whereas the latter frequently neglects to account for the intentional use of these sites. By either bracketing social structures or eradicating the reflexive agency of users, neither of these perspectives fully account for the dialectical relationship between agency and structure. This state of affairs could to some extent be explained by the ideological assumptions by which these perspectives are fundamentally marked. Positioning Web 2.0 applications as mechanisms of utility, the former perspective provides an understanding which often echoes what Couldry terms the 'individualizing rhetoric of neoliberalism' (2011, p. 497). Mainly drawing on critical theory, the latter perspective, in contrast, brings forth a fairly pessimistic comprehension of these phenomena by highlighting the structural conditions of their being used.

While it is important to recognise that SNS allow for a certain amount of interactivity along with certain exploitative practices, neither of these divergent approaches account for how SNS assume a functional position within the social realm. Earlier in this paper, it was argued that the very possibility to interact depends on the presence of other actors as well as the social space in which they are situated. For this reason, it is decisive to acknowledge that the back-end processing of harvested personal an interactional data not only serves for the purpose of exploitation, but also for structuring the social spaces in which user activity takes place. Following this line of thought, SNS intervene in the social realm by mediating social and symbolic content while at the same time regulating, and to some extent structuring that very content. Thus, not only do these sites mediate and process the informational exchange between users, but also affect the structure of the social situation by altering the visibility and spatial framing of other users and their shared information. The above discussion points at the difficulties attached to the divergent approaches towards SNS and illuminates the need for striking a balance between individual-oriented and system-oriented agency. Not only would it be erroneous to ascribe agency to either the individual user or to back-end mechanisms, but such a misdirected focus fails to account for the dialectical relationship between front-end characteristics and back-end mechanisms. It is clear that these core aspects of SNS are acting in concert, thus altering the conditions for the social situation. When these matters are taken into account, the need for a conceptual reconfiguration of SNS becomes clear.

As the above discussion demonstrates, SNS mediate social interaction while at the same time assuming the role of a communicative counterpart that intervenes in the social situation. For this reason, these sites are better understood in terms of social intermediaries. Conceptually, the term social intermediaries allows for an exploration of how the connection between front-end characteristics and back-end mechanisms provokes changes in the social dynamics. Importantly, social intermediaries provide the infrastructural circumstances for social interaction while simultaneously conditioning the spatial distribution of social occurrences through the user interface. Social intermediaries thus function as structuring links between actors in the sense that they do not simply deliver social or symbolic content from one point to the other but also, which is of pivotal importance, structure the content in various ways. This means that social intermediaries are not only situated between actors, but are also agents that intervene in social interactions and exchanges from that intermediate position. In this sense, social intermediaries enter the social realm as actors fuelled by back-end processing of personal and interactional data. Hence, social intermediaries do not only allow for a certain amount of interactivity or engage in exploitative use of personal and interactional data, but rather enter the social situation by altering the front-end characteristics through a constant back-end processing of data. In consequence, social intermediaries provoke changes at the level of social arithmetic, which could be understood as an 'arithmetically definable quantitative determination of social formations' (Pyyhtinen, 2009, p. 109). This means that social intermediaries assume a functional position in the social realm of which they form a part at a given moment in time and space. Importantly, social intermediaries do not only operate in the social realm, but also tend to coincide with that realm in which social actors are embedded in relationships of mutual exchange.

At the level of social arithmetic, social intermediaries are characterised by an in-betweenness amongst social actors, and thus alter the conditions for communication and social interaction by introducing a third actor into the social situation. In this sense, social intermediaries partake in the social exchange while simultaneously providing the basis for a regulation governing that very exchange. In order to grasp the complexity of these processes, there is a need to illuminate the relational and intermediary mode of the social realm. An important foundation for this line of thought is found in Simmel's (2009/1908) account of the 'social', which he locates in the relational interplay between actors. The 'social' should thus not be understood as 'a static object but a fluctuating, dynamic reciprocity between individuals' (Pyyhtinen, 2009, p. 114). Such an understanding of the 'social' highlights the importance of considering the number of actors involved in a specific social situation. Distinguishing between the social forms of the dyad and the triad, Simmel argues that the arrival of a third actor brings about fundamental changes in the social situation. '[T]he entry of the third', Simmel writes, 'means transformation, reconciliation, abandonment of absolute opposition—of course occasionally even the instigation of such' (2009/1908, p. 101). As a social form, the triad allows for certain kinds of group formations that would not be possible without the arrival of the third. In his exploration of Simmel's account of the 'social', Pyyhtinen maintains that '[t]he "third" not only interrupts the supposedly immediate relation between the two elements of the dyad, but it is also capable of transforming it into a completely new figure: a social whole, a "we", which obtains a supra-individual life independent of the individuals' (2009, p. 108). Elaborating this idea further, Pyyhtinen suggests that, 'in the twosome the individuals are confronted only by one another /.../ but with the arrival of the third, the individuals may have a relation with the relation itself' (2009, pp. 117–118). Entering the social situation as a third actor, social intermediaries assume a complex functional position. Not only do they form the infrastructural condition of social interaction, but also alter the relationship between the other actors involved. As Pyyhtinen argues, 'the possibility of the dyad is conditioned by the third, and the actions of the third, in turn, already presuppose the dyad' (2009, p. 119). In consequence, as was pointed out by Jarrett (2008) earlier in this paper, social intermediaries not only allow agential subjects to engage in various forms of social interaction, but rather install a certain desire and capacity to interact. We are thus dealing with a complex interplay between front-end characteristics and back-end processes, through which a social and spatial structuring is taking place. Returning to Pyyhtinen's idea that the third enables a relationship with 'the relation itself', it is important to note that the basis for such a relationship is formed by the back-end processing of harvested personal and interactional data. Hence, when social intermediaries enter the social situation as a third actor, they provide an informational feedback based upon interactions that have taken place at an earlier temporal stage.

Conclusion

Drawing on an exploration of two streams of research, the above discussion has pointed out that contemporary research on SNS tends to locate agency at quite different levels. In order to establish an understanding of the social dynamics of these sites, there is clearly a need for a reconfigured conceptual apparatus. Drawing on Simmel's understanding of the 'social' it has been argued that the term 'social intermediaries' is more precise than the concept of SNS since it casts light on the functional position that these sites occupy in the social realm, rather than illuminating a particular relationship between user and system. In overall terms, social intermediaries are located in the tension between individual-oriented and system-oriented agency and intervene in the social realm as agents on own behalf. This implies that social intermediaries should not only be regarded as sites and applications that provide a means for individual pursuits or function as instruments for harvesting personal information but rather as distinct and somewhat independent entities. Understood in this way, social intermediaries enter the social situation as a third actor, while at the same time providing the infrastructural condition for that very situation. In contrast to the prevailing understanding of SNS, the term social intermediaries allows for an understanding of these phenomena as services that facilitate the establishment and sustainment of social ties between social actors. At the same time, social intermediaries enter the social realm as agential mechanisms that assume a functional position between actors wherefrom an exchange of social and symbolic content is facilitated. Furthermore, social intermediaries partake in such exchanges by means of regulatory standards and other forms of actions possible to undertake through the processing of harvested personal and interactional data. Understood in such a way, social intermediaries are always acting from a position between individuals while at the same time rendering themselves and their interventions more or less invisible. Social intermediaries thus always consist of both front-end characteristics and back-end mechanisms that, acting in concert with and towards the user, gain momentum by taking up a position as a third actor in the field of communication and social interaction. This implies that the term social intermediaries bears a possibility to theorise the social dynamics of contemporary online phenomena from a perspective that strikes a balance between individual-oriented and system-oriented agency while simultaneously transcending the rhetorics, which are often attached to interpretations of these phenomena. In this sense, such a conceptualisation of social intermediaries provides an opportunity to shift focus towards the social realm as such, which facilitates the establishment of an understanding that can be critically related to a larger theoretical whole.

Acknowledgements

This research was supported by *The Bank of Sweden Tercentenary Foundation* (Riksbankens Jubileumsfond). The author is grateful to the editor of the journal and the anonymous referees for constructive comments and suggestions.

Notes

1. The concept of social intermediaries has been used elsewhere, most notably by Kahn (2010) for whom the term indicates various web-based tools for enabling portable identities across websites. In contrast, this paper suggests that the concepts of social intermediaries can be used as an alternative to SNS that allows for an understanding of the functional position that such intermediate agents assume.
2. The term front-end refers to the visible parts of Web 2.0 applications (i.e. the user interface) through which various kinds of informational input is made possible. In contrast, the term back-end is used to describe the invisible underlying mechanisms by which the same informational input is stored in databases and processed in order to provide a basis for the structuring of front-end experiences.
3. At the time of writing this paper (June 15, 2011), the web page to which Scholtz refers does not include O'Reilly's comment. A similar comment from the same author is however to be found at http://radar.oreilly.com/2007/10/todays-web-30-nonsense-blogsto.html (accessed 15 June 2011).

References

Acquisti, A. & Gross, R. (2006) Imagined communities: awareness, information sharing, and privacy on the Facebook, in: G. Danezis & P. Golle (Eds) *Privacy enhancing technologies, 6th International Workshop, PET 2006* (New York, Springer).

Allen, M. (2008) Web 2.0: an argument against convergence, *First Monday*, 13. Available online at: http://www.uic.edu/htbin/cgiwrap/bin/ojs/index.php/fm/article/view/2139/1946

Andrejevic, M. (2011) Surveillance and alienation in the online economy, *Surveillance & Society*, 8, 278–287.

Beer, D. (2008) Social network(ing) sites... revisiting the story so far: a response to danah boyd & Nicole Ellison, *Journal of Computer-Mediated Communication*, 13, 516–529.

Beer, D. & Burrows, R. (2007) Sociology and, of and in Web 2.0: some initial considerations, *Sociological Research Online*, 12, 17.

Beer, D. & Burrows, R. (2010) Consumption, prosumption and participatory web cultures: an introduction, *Journal of Consumer Culture*, 10, 3–12.

Benedikt, M. (2000/1991) Cyberspace: first steps, in: D. Bell & B. M. Kennedy (Eds) *The cybercultures reader* (London, Routledge).

Bird, E. S. (2011) Are we all produsers now? *Cultural Studies*, 25, 502–516.

boyd, D. (2008) Why youth (heart) social network sites: the role of networked publics in teenage social life, in: D. Buckingham (Ed.) *Youth, identity, and digital media* (Cambridge, MA, The MIT Press).

boyd, D. M. & Ellison, N. B. (2007) Social network sites: definition, history, and scholarship, *Journal of Computer-Mediated Communication*, 13, 210–230.

Bruns, A. (2008) *Blogs, Wikipedia, second life, and beyond: from production to produsage* (New York, Peter Lang).

Castells, M. (2009) *Communication power* (Oxford & New York, Oxford University Press).

Couldry, N. (2011) More sociology, more culture, more politics: or, a modest proposal for 'convergence' studies, *Cultural Studies*, 25, 487–501.

Dean, J. (2010) *Blog theory: feedback and capture in the circuits of drive* (Cambridge, Polity Press).

Debatin, B., Lovejoy, J. P., Horn, A.-K. & Hughes, B. N. (2009) Facebook and online privacy: attitudes, behaviors, and unintended consequences, *Journal of Computer-Mediated Communication*, 15, 83–108.

Dwyer, C., Hiltz, S. R. & Passerini, K. (2007) Trust and privacy concern within social networking sites: a comparison of Facebook and MySpace, *Proceedings of the Thirteenth Americas Conference on Information Systems*, Keystone, Colorado, August 9–12.

Ellison, N. B., Steinfield, C. & Lampe, C. (2007) The benefits of Facebook 'friends': social capital and college students' use of online social network sites, *Journal of Computer-Mediated Communication*, 12, 1143–1168.

Fuchs, C. (2008) *Internet and society: social theory in the information age* (London & New York, Routledge).

Fuchs, C. (2010) Labor in informational capitalism and on the internet, *Information Society*, 26, 179–179.

Fuchs, C. (2011) Web 2.0, prosumption, and surveillance, *Surveillance & Society*, 8, 288–309.

Gauntlett, D. (2011) *Making is connecting: the social meaning of creativity, from DIY and knitting to YouTube and Web 2.0* (Cambridge, Polity Press).

Gehl, R. W. (2011) The archive and the processor: the internal logic of Web 2.0, *New Media & Society*, 1–17.

Giddens, A. (1991) *Modernity and self-identity: self and society in the late modern age* (Stanford, CA, Stanford University Press).

Jarrett, K. (2008) Interactivity is evil! A critical investigation of Web 2.0, *First Monday*, 13. Available online at: http://www.uic.edu/htbin/cgiwrap/bin/ojs/index.php/fm/article/view/2140/1947

Jenkins, H. (2008) *Convergence culture: where old and new media collide* (New York, New York University Press).

Kahn, D. H. (2010) Social intermediaries: creating a more responsible web through portable identity, cross-web reputation, and code-backed norms, *The Columbia Science and Technology Review*, XI, 176–242.

Kincaid, J. (2010) EdgeRank: the secret sauce that makes Facebook's news feed tick, *TechCrunch*, Available online at: http://techcrunch.com/2010/04/22/facebook-edgerank (accessed 1 April 2012).

Lampe, C., Ellison, N. & Steinfield, C. (2006) A face(book) in the crowd: social searching vs. social browsing, *CSCW '06: Proceedings of the 2006 20th anniversary conference on Computer supported cooperative work*, ACM, 167–170.

McKenna, K. Y. A., Green, A. S. & Gleason, M. E. J. (2002) Relationship formation on the internet: what's the big attraction? *Journal of Social Issues*, 58, 9–31.

McStay, A. (2011) Profiling phorm: an autopoietic approach to the audience-as-commodity, *Surveillance & Society*, 8, 310–322.

Mead, G. H. (1934) *Mind, self, and society: from the standpoint of a social behaviorist* (Chicago, IL, University of Chicago Press).

Petersen, S. M. (2008) Loser generated content: from participation to exploitation, *First Monday*, 13. Available online at: http://www.uic.edu/htbin/cgiwrap/bin/ojs/index.php/fm/article/view/2141/1948

Pyyhtinen, O. (2009) Being-with: Georg Simmel's sociology of association, *Theory, Culture & Society*, 26, 108–128.

Rheingold, H. (1995) *The virtual community: finding connection in a computerized world* (London, Minerva).

Ritzer, G. & Jurgenson, N. (2010) Production, consumption, prosumption: the nature of capitalism in the age of the digital 'prosumer', *Journal of Consumer Culture*, 10, 13–36.
Scholz, T. (2008) Market ideology and the myths of Web 2.0, *First Monday*, 13. Available online at: http://www.uic.edu/htbin/cgiwrap/bin/ojs/index.php/fm/article/view/2138/1945
Shirky, C. (2009) *Here comes everybody: how change happens when people come together* (London, Penguin Books).
Shirky, C. (2010) *Cognitive surplus: creativity and generosity in a connected age* (New York, The Penguin Press).
Silver, D. (2008) History, hype, and hope: an afterward, *First Monday*, 13. Available online at: http://www.uic.edu/htbin/cgiwrap/bin/ojs/index.php/fm/article/view/2143/1950
Simmel, G. (2009/1908) *Sociology: inquiries into the construction of social forms* (Leiden, Brill).
Stutzman, F. (2006) An evaluation of identity-sharing behavior in social network communities, *International Digital and Media Arts Journal*, 3.
Terranova, T. (2004) *Network culture: politics for the information age* (London, Pluto Press).
Thrift, N. (2005) *Knowing capitalism* (London, Sage).
Toffler, A. (1980) *The third wave* (New York, William Morrow).
Turkle, S. (1995) *Life on the screen: identity in the age of the internet* (London, Phoenix).
Valenzuela, S., Park, N. & Kee, K. F. (2009) Is there social capital in a social network site?: Facebook use and college students' life satisfaction, trust, and participation, *Journal of Computer-Mediated Communication*, 14, 875–901.
Vergeer, M. & Pelzer, B. (2009) Consequences of media and Internet use for offline and online network capital and well-being. A causal model approach, *Journal of Computer-Mediated Communication*, 15, 189–210.
Zimmer, M. (2008a) The externalities of Search 2.0: the emerging privacy threats when the drive for the perfect search engine meets Web 2.0, *First Monday*, 13. Available online at: http://www.uic.edu/htbin/cgiwrap/bin/ojs/index.php/fm/article/view/2136/1944
Zimmer, M. (2008b) Preface: critical perspectives on Web 2.0, *First Monday*, 13. Available online at: http://www.uic.edu/htbin/cgiwrap/bin/ojs/index.php/fm/article/view/2137/1943

Musical tastes in the Web 2.0: the importance of network dynamics

Kostas Kasaras, George Michael Klimis and Martha Michailidou

Department of Communication, Media and Culture, Panteion University, Athens, Greece

Information and communication technologies and the technologies of Web 2.0 have brought a revolution that acts as a prelude of creative destruction for the incumbents in most sectors of the economy. One of the most affected sectors is that of the music industry. After a brief discussion of the cultural industries and the significance of the music industry, the paper turns to theoretical approaches to Social Networks and their analysis, and especially the ways in which social influence has traditionally been conceptualised. It then offers an examination of Salganik and Watts' web-based experiments for the study of collective social dynamics in cultural markets, and proposes a new experimental design for the examination of the potentially novel forms of influence developing in the ecology of the Web 2.0.

Introduction

The year 1993 is one of the landmark years in the history of the world. It is the year the Mosaic browser was released, bringing a cataclysmic change. Enabling the consumer to take control of the Internet by a GUI (Graphical User Interface) was akin to the change brought by mass production by Ford. It led to the democratisation of the internet, up until then an 'arcane' network appealing to a handful of scientists or those few that felt comfortable with writing commands in text-based environments.

In the years that followed, and especially in the new millennium, the social web, in particular, and the technologies and applications that come under the name Web 2.0 facilitated peer-to-peer (P2P) interaction and socialisation of agents online, and have changed dramatically the way consumers interact and behave online.

The revolution brought about by so-called Information and Communication Technologies (ICTs) in general, and the Web 2.0 in particular, can be understood through the notion of creative destruction conceptualised by Schumpeter (1950, p. 85), as a reversal of the established order brought about by the agents of change, the entrepreneurs. Entrepreneurship in Schumpeter (1934, p. 66) is defined as 'new combinations of inputs... [Which] cover the following five cases: (1) The introduction of a new good... or a new quality product; (2) The introduction of a new production method...; (3) Opening a new market...; (4) The conquest of a new source of supply for raw materials...; [and] (5) The implementation of a new organisation of any industry'. Historical examples of creative destruction were the invention of print, the democratisation of the car by Henry Ford, and the development of the personal computer (PC) by IBM. In all these cases, the consequences of the revolution were disastrous for the incumbents, those, that is, who held prominent positions in sectors that were destroyed.

Many scholars tried to dissect the internet's effect on industries or companies at the time (see, for example, Tapscott, 1996; Porter, 2001), and a good number talked about potential business models that would enable entrepreneurs to profit from what appeared to be the new gold rush (Afuah & Tucci, 2001), albeit with mixed results, since Nasdaq's crash brought an end to what seemed to be an irrational exuberance.

One of the industries that were at the forefront of that revolution was the music industry. The sheer complexity of issues that confronted incumbents and entrepreneurs alike and the ease of access and magnitude of demand by consumers were overwhelming. Music on Demand was probably the first service developed for the Internet. Such is the importance of the music industry that other industries (banking, insurance, even shipping) were and still are watching it, using it as the miners did the canary, testing the mineshaft before they could proceed. Lester Thurow confirms: 'Every business firm should imagine that they are in the music business... It is your problem in the sense that every industry is going to face a similar problem even if the problem emerges more slowly than in the case of music' (preface to Hax & Wilde, 2001).

A definition of the cultural industries and the significance of the music industry

The Web 2.0's killer application is P2P file sharing. This type of sharing of music is viewed by the recording industry as a nuisance at best, as an illegitimate activity worthy of prosecution at worst. The problem of the recording industry (an industry which should be understood as being a subsection of the music industry) rests on the erosion of the comfortable profits enjoyed in bygone eras. As more and more Internet users download files from P2P networks and music accounts for around 50% of all files shared using these applications, music becomes the most shared content of all. The recording industry has responded to this threat with copyright infringement lawsuits against song swappers. Researchers such as Liebowitz (2005) are adamant that

P2P is detrimental to the whole of the music industry, as it negatively affects music sales. In contrast, Oberholzer-Gee and Strumpf (2007) argue that this effect is negligible. Others, such as Blackburn (2004), argue that illegal file sharing has beneficial effects to 'ex ante unknown artists' and detrimental to the 'ex ante known artists'.[1] While the jury is still out on this issue, few research studies have actually focused on the ways in which consumers' attitudes, beliefs and tastes are formed in this new, networked, environment. This paper aims to provide a starting point towards filling this gap.

Of course, the debate on the definition, characteristics and socio-political implications of the cultural industries is a long and fruitful one, from Adorno's (1991) conceptualisation of the culture industries as an industrial apparatus for the mass production of standardised cultural goods addressed to the masses to the British cultural studies approach which emphasised culture as a terrain of meaning-making and appropriation. Contemporary discussions of the *creative* industries—in policy (Department for Culture, Media and Sport—DCMS, 1998) and academic research (Caves, 2000; Cunningham, 2004; Potts *et al.*, 2008)—mark a transition to understandings of culture as an entrepreneurially driven and privately funded industry (Klimis & Wallis, 2009). Beyond the classic definitions of cultural/creative industries, Kretschmer *et al.* (1999, p. S62) have proposed that an industry is cultural when: there is oversupply of goods candidate for commercialisation; the quality of goods is unclear; consumers of these goods form specific networks; the demand for goods is reversed in a cyclical manner

Leaving aside the analysis of the last element—the demand for goods and how fashion shapes it in a cyclical manner—a task we can devote another paper to, but without underestimating its contribution to our understanding of cultural industries, we will now briefly turn to the three other elements of the definition.

Oversupply is due to the vanity of creators and the low barriers to entry in cultural industries. Anyone can become an artist, while it is considerably more difficult (and less lucrative) to become a medical doctor, a lawyer or an engineer. Besides that, oversupply can also be a strategy used by producers (publishers, record labels etc.) to deal with the problem of uncertainty. Oversupply is dealt with filtering mechanisms in the creative industries. Functions such as the A&R (Artist and Repertoire) in a recording label, editors in publishing, and talent scouts in the mass media such as radio and TV can act as cultural intermediaries (du Gay & Pryke, 2002) and gatekeepers, providing 'expert' opinions aiming to direct the audience to particular cultural goods and attempting to influence and shape consumer taste.

Quality Uncertainty is an inherent characteristic of the cultural industry since its goods are what we call credence goods, i.e. goods where the quality cannot be determined even after the consumption of the good.[2] As argued by Kretschmer *et al.* (1999), cultural property creates a failure in the market. This quality problem gives rise to the creation of entities that Emons (1997) describes as 'fraudulent experts', who exploit the inability of consumers to discern quality and offer appropriate services. Such experts are art critics, for example, and all kinds of producers who act as gatekeepers in the system.

The rise, in the past decade, of horizontal and complex networks of music production, distribution and consumption in the Web 2.0 has been widely discussed in communications and media studies. One of the main issues discussed was whether the traditionally singular expertise of cultural intermediaries (Bourdieu, 1984) with the related mechanisms of mediation and gate-keeping which had prevailed in the twentieth century culture of the mass media,[3] shaping the practices of distribution and consumption of cultural goods, may be replaced in the Web 2.0 with mechanisms of collaborative filtering or social recommendation sites which will eschew traditional mechanisms of filtering and influence.

From experts to networks in the music industry

Consumers participate in one or more *networks* that distribute and diffuse cultural goods as well as information. Consumer networking creates phenomena of social contagion and increasing returns. Typical phenomena of feedback caused by networks are found to apply primarily to the binary decisions consumers make in markets of information technology, for example, in a battle of standards (Arthur, 1996). This leads to 'winner takes all' markets (Frank & Cook, 1995), where an endogenous and dynamic self-reinforcing feedback cycle realises a 'success breeds success' trajectory for the product and/or the artist.

It is consumers themselves that drive these phenomena. There are many theories in economics on 'herd behaviour' (a rich recent literature can be found in the layman's approach given by Earls, 2007). In the case of cultural industries and markets, in particular, where, as mentioned before, the quality is uncertain, phenomena such as that of herd behaviour or fad and fashion are more prevalent than in other industries. While lock-in is not as predominant as in the software industry (a consumer can listen to different artists and kinds of music while one mainly uses one operating system for their PC), these networks are subject to positive network externalities (Katz & Shapiro, 1985), which means that the more people consume a cultural product the more beneficial it becomes for the next potential consumer. The value of a network of, say, people who have watched a movie and are talking socially about this at various locations (work, entertainment etc.) grows exponentially as more nodes (i.e. people) are added to the network.

Conceptual roots of social network analysis

Today, Web 2.0 social networks diffuse in rapid numbers around the world and people tend to spend increasing amounts of time on them each day.[4] However, despite the fact that the hype about social networks has only recently become a worldwide trend, the network concept is not new. In fact 'social networks—real or virtual—are collections of human communities' (Petroczi et al., 2010, p. 39) and, consequently, many authors argue that the dawn of social network analysis (SNA) was created at the very beginning of sociology.

The roots of SNA can be found as far back as the 1930s, in the rise of organisational research and the development of sociometry by Jacob Levy Moreno. Moreno was the first who elaborated methodological tools that could be considered precursors to contemporary social network analysis models, systematically recording and analysing 'social interaction in small groups, especially classrooms and work groups' (Zhang, 2010, p. 9). Moreno's work used a multimethodological framework in order to chart the ways in which group relations formed people's actions and, by extension, their psychological development. In addition, Moreno's research was innovative in arguing that sociometries can be represented by graphical illustrations, where actors are represented by points and their relations by lines and paths.

About the same time two young mathematicians from Budapest, Paul Erdos and Alfred Renyi, started working on their 'random network theory', which aspired to represent a worldwide theory of networks. Their theory succeeded in dominating scientific conceptualisations of networks (Barabasi, 2002, p. 23), and ambitious projects were later on developed at the University of Harvard. More specifically, the main contribution of Harvard's scholars (Lloyd Warner and Elton Mayo) was the deconstruction of networks into subgroups (cliques—clusters—blocks) and the charting of their structure and relations, through the use of sociometric methods. Warner and Mayo came to the conclusion that the social configuration of modern societies is shaped by the interplay of sub-groups (cliques) such as the family, church and clubs; they therefore defined cliques as the key point in their theoretical model. This was further elaborated by Davis *et al.* (1941), who, in their 'Deep South Project', showed that cliques are organised in three layers, depending on the intensity and frequency of their member relations. The first one was named 'the core' and it represented those actors that communicated frequently and more intensely. The second layer consisted of those who occasionally interact with the core, but never as a group, and the third layer contained those who participated rarely and were thought as almost non-members.

Despite the fact that early social network theory was produced by several scholars in the United States and abroad, there are no signs of exchanged knowledge or any other type of communication. Sociologist and social psychologist George Gaspar Homans proposed, in his 1950 publication 'The Human Group', the 'threefold classification' model in order to ground his basic idea that modern social theory should be based on the understanding of sub-groups and the interactions inside them. Human interactions vary in frequency, duration and direction, while more intense interplay results in greater attachment and the opposite.

Stanley Milgram conceptualised, in 1967, one of the most famous experiments and classic references in psychology. His aim was to discover how many steps were required for someone to reach a completely unknown person in a different state, by sending him/her a postcard (indirectly). He discovered 'that the median number of intermediate persons was 5.5, a very small number indeed… Round it up to 6, however, and you get the famous "six degrees of separation"' (Barabasi, 2002, p. 29). Milgram's findings supported Erdos and Renyi's earlier argument, showing that there is a path connecting every person in the world, a path with six stops. The experiment was repeated by Duncan Watts in 2001, using emails instead of postcards. Over 60,000 people from 166 different countries participated, while the 'targets' were random people from all over the world. In order to analyse how 'tight' a network is, Watts proposed the Clustering Coefficient, which measures the degree to which nodes in a graph tend to cluster together.

Another important reference point in social network analysis comes from Mark Granovetter's (1974) research. The research concentrated on 300 professionals from Boston who had changed employment in the few months preceding the experiment, investigating the network of friends they had sought in order to find their new occupations. It was observed that 56% of them had found their new jobs through connections described as simple acquaintances. As Zhang argues, by 'using a network perspective, Mark Granovetter put forward the theory of the "strength-of-weak-ties"... Because cliques have a tendency to have more homogeneous opinions and common traits, individuals in the same cliques would also know more or less what the other members know. To gain new information and opinion, people often look beyond the clique to their other friends and acquaintances' (2010, p. 17). This points out to the importance of bridges *between* different networks, bridges being weak ties which may connect different groups (Freidkin, 1980, pp. 411–412).

The mechanics of influence: from opinion leaders and intermediaries to network dynamics

One of the major preoccupations underlying the development of early social network theory has been the question of social influence. Foundational in this approach has been the rise of 'organizational' research carried out by Lazarsfeld and his associates at the Bureau of Applied Social Research, one of the most methodologically inventive and empirically sustained attempts at investigating the mechanisms of social influence characteristic of US post-war society.

The Bureau's research on the formation of US public opinion on the eve of the 1940 presidential election (Lazarsfeld *et al.*, 1944) studied the ways in which public opinion regarding the presidential candidates was formed. The study used panel interviews to chart the factors and people which according to the participants were responsible for the formation of their opinion on public affairs, placing emphasis on the investigation of the possible effects of media coverage and advertising campaigns on the formation of the public's views on the candidates and, through this, on their eventual voting preference. The study argued that media effects were mediated through 'opinion leaders', persons of high standing in the local communities who had more exposure to the debates concerning public affairs in the media, and would therefore act as intermediaries to the rest of the people.

This study, together with the subsequent study on *Personal Influence* formed the basis of what came to be known as the two-step flow model of communication, according to which 'ideas, often, seem to flow from radio and print to opinion leaders and from them to the less active sections of the population' (Katz & Lazarsfeld, 2009 [1955], p. 32). The model broke with the communication paradigms prevalent at the time in US communications research, which either analysed communication from a technical standpoint as the linear transmission of information from a source to a destination or as a fundamentally psychological process of message as stimulus and reception as response to this stimulus (Katz, 2009, p. xxii), and introduced the notion of limited media effects.

This model, in turn, acted as the conceptual and methodological prerequisite for the study of diffusion. Coleman *et al.*'s (1957) study of the spread of a new medicine in a group of medical practitioners was seminal in this respect, as it attempted to chart the differential significance of sales representatives, advertising, medical journals and interpersonal influence for the doctors' choice of medicine, and measure it through the use of sociometric techniques. The model set by this research led to Everett Roger's (2003 [1962]) study of the implementation and the diffusion of, among others, consumer products in a new technological environment. In his book *The Diffusion of Innovations* Rogers (2003) proposes a model for what he termed 'diffusion studies', by which he attempted to explain how innovations (ideas, behaviours or objects) are taken up in a population or, in other words, how they get perceived as new and adopted by the audience. The book also provided a typology of consumer tendencies towards innovation, categorizing users as innovators, early adopters, early majority, late majority, and laggards.

The importance of the Bureau's investigations of personal influence and of its model of media effects as mediated through personal influence in providing some of the conceptual roots for contemporary social network analysis cannot be overestimated. As Katz argues, in a retrospective account of the importance of Lazarsfeld's work and his collaboration with him, 'Those who have continued in the study of persuasion have, on the whole, reiterated the Lazarsfeld findings of limited effects, while contributing to the further specification of the conditions under which the media may indeed affect change in people... Lazarsfeldians have taken selectivity and interpersonal relations as points of departure in expanding persuasion studies into the diffusion of innovation' (2001, p. 271).

However, the process of diffusion in a hierarchically structured world, where social influence operates on the basis of strength of well established social relationships and, more importantly, on the basis of the presumed elevated status, however local, of opinion leaders, may differ considerably from processes of contagion which become possible in the highly complex social environments of the contemporary Web 2.0. The question then becomes how to study processes of social contagion in contemporary Web 2.0 environments without presuming the high significance, and therefore, the highly influential capacity, of opinion leaders, which act, in the case of music, as, certified cultural intermediaries. For this reason, we turn to the experimental method, in order to identify the forces shaping musical taste and the consumption of music in a social network, being able to investigate in real time and in an actual network setting the mechanisms of influence which develop as part of indigenous network dynamics. After a brief section on the analytical tools used in SNA, we will turn to contemporary applications of the experimental method in the study of unpredictability in the formation of musical taste, and, in the last section of the paper, we shall sketch out our proposed experiment in more detail.

Analytical tools used in SNA

As discussed in the previous section, sustained attempts towards network theorisations of social activity developed well before the rise of computer mediated communication (CMC), let alone the Web 2.0. As a consequence, developing appropriate analytical tools for SNA in the CMC era has been a dynamic process, testing already established notions and practices in a new technological and communicative environment.

In order to develop a network analysis, one has to be familiar with the commonly used terminology. According to Zhang, the most important concepts in SNA are ties, density, centrality, cliques and homophily/heterophily. 'Ties or links connect two and more nodes in a graph' (2010, p. 12) and can be direct or indirect, binary or valued. The route between two ties is called 'a path'. 'Nodes or actors may be directly connected by a line, or they may be indirectly connected through a sequence of lines. A sequence of lines in a graph is a "walk"; and a walk in which each point and each line are distinct is called a path. The concept of the path is, after those of the node and the line, one of the most basic of all graph theoretical concepts. The length of a path is measured by the number of lines which make it up. The distance between two nodes is the length of the shortest path (the "geodesic") which connects them' (Zhang, 2010, p. 13). Density refers to the general level of linkage among the points in a graph. Clique is a term that describes the existence of a sub-group inside a network. In a clique, each node is connected to any other node in the subgraph.

Another very important concept that identifies and often shapes a sub-group is homophily.[5] 'Homophily explains group composition in terms of the similarity of members' characteristics: the extent to which pairs of individuals are similar in terms of certain attributes, such as age, gender, education, or lifestyle' (Brown, 2007, p. 5). While homophily functions as a vicious circle between nodes in a network by maintaining and reinforcing the flow of information, heterophilous communication can also function in important ways in a network, as Rogers (2003) argues, given that heterophilous links may connect two different cliques. This way, weak ties are created, which, Rogers (2003), following Granovetter, argues are necessary for the wide diffusion of innovations.

Probably the most important role in a social network is played by the degree of the centrality of a node. As Ortiz-Arroyo argues 'centrality describes an actor's relative position within the context of his or her social network... Nodes with high degree centrality have higher probability of receiving and transmitting whatever information flows in the network. For this reason, high degree centrality nodes are considered to have influence over a larger number of nodes and/or are capable of communicating quickly with the nodes in their neighbourhood' (2010, p. 28). In conclusion, centrality is a key concept in order for someone to identify and analyse the important nodes in a graph and its basic measures are: *degree, between-ness and closeness centrality.*

The measure of degree refers to 'the number of direct connections a node has. Degree centrality is the sum of all other actors who are directly connected to ego. It signifies activity or popularity' (Zhang, 2010, p. 14). Between-ness is a way of counting popularity as it 'is the number of times a node connects pairs of other nodes, who otherwise would not be able to reach one another. It is a measure of the potential for control, as an actor who is high in "between-ness" is able to act as a gatekeeper controlling the flow of resources... between the alters that he or she connects' (Zhang, 2010, p. 14). Closeness centrality measures how close a node is to all others inside a network.

Measuring inequality in unpredictable cultural markets: contemporary experiments

Between 2006 and 2009, Salganik and Watts and their associates carried out a number of web-based experiments for the study of collective social dynamics in cultural markets (Salganik *et al.*, 2006; Salganik & Watts, 2009). Their aim was to investigate the role of social influence on the decision making process in cultural products by using a 'multiple-worlds' experimental design that contributes to the isolation of the 'casual effect on an individual-level mechanism on collective social outcomes' and 'gain new insights into the role of individual behaviour on collective outcomes' (2009, p. 439). Salganik and Watts (2009) revisit the classic question of influence, which has been, as discussed in previous sections of this paper, a constant analytical and methodological conundrum throughout the history of media studies.

As discussed in a previous section of this paper, cultural industries are completely unpredictable in terms of attempting to forecast success. Because of this, many researchers tend to use bisectional approaches to conceptualise cultural products as fundamentally different from other consumer goods. Kretschmer *et al.* proposed a dichotomy of experience and credence goods; they argued that for the former 'quality can only be learned after use', while for the latter people tend to be '*dependent on what other people think*, before consumption' (1999, p. S63). In a similar vein, Smith *et al.* proposed a similar approach toward shopping objectives, arguing that they can be utilitarian and/or hedonic; in their view, for products which are primarily hedonic 'consumers will rely on the level of perceived rapport or closeness shared with recommenders to judge their trustworthiness' (2005, p. 17). In this context, Salganik and Watts attempt to deconstruct the following puzzle: 'If hits are different in some way, why do experts have such difficulty in identifying these products ahead of time? Rather than looking for an explanation of this puzzle at the level of the individual—either industry executives or consumers—we will argue that the inequality and unpredictability of success, both group-level properties, arise from a process of social influence at the individual level' (2009, p. 442).

In their latest publication in 2009, Salganik and Watts published the methodology and the results of three web-based experiments that they conducted. In total, there were 2930 participants who listened, rated and downloaded 48 songs by upcoming bands. They succeeded in analysing what the sociologist Morris Zeldich had wished to in 1969, studying a whole 'army' in a laboratory by using facilities that only new technologies and the Web 2.0 could provide. They organised each experiment and made small but important qualitative changes in each one of them. More specifically, in the first experiment—without the participants' knowledge—the researchers used multiple 'worlds' in which each participant was randomly placed. 'Upon arrival to the website, participants were randomly assigned into either the independent condition, where they had no information about the behaviour of others, or the social influence condition, within which they were also assigned to a specific "world" where they had information about the behaviour of those in their world, but not those in the other worlds' (2009, p. 444). Within each 'world', songs were randomly presented to each participant, who were asked to rate them on a scale of 1 star ('I hate it') to 5 stars ('I love it'). Moreover, the design of the experiment provided the opportunity for each participant to download a song before proceeding to listen to the remaining songs. The download counts were updated accurately, and in real time, and presented only to the socially influenced participants, whereas participants in the independent condition received no such information.

The other two experiments they conducted had approximately the same structure but two main differences. In Experiment 1, 'songs were presented in a 16 × 3 grid not sorted by popularity, while in Experiment 2, the songs were presented in a single-column format sorted by popularity. In the independent condition of both Experiments, the songs were presented in the same format, but without any information about popularity and in a random order' (2009, p. 446). Experiment 3 differentiated by including participants who were older, more male than female, more international and who 'listened to twice as many songs' (2009, p. 453) than those who partook in the previous experiments.

In all experiments, they found that in their eight social influence worlds there is an exhibition of greater inequality—meaning that popular songs were more popular and unpopular songs were less popular—than the world in which individuals make decisions independently, while 'every social influence in Experiment 2 was more unequal than the most unequal in Experiment 1' (2009, p. 448).

Web experimental network design after Salganik and Watts

To summarise the results of the three experiments, one could argue that Salganik and Watts succeeded in demonstrating a fascinating approach to all theories that support the idea of the non-rationality of choice in cultural products and manifest the applicability of social influence. In their words 'our explanation, therefore, takes the constructed preferences view of human psychology seriously and adds to it a social component; that is, we propose that expressed preferences are influenced by the observed actions of others, as well as by psychological features of the decision context, such as framing, anchoring, and availability' (2009, p. 442).

However, the experimental model that Salganik and Watts created does not support the analysis of social influence as a result of participants' interplay. As they also acknowledge, limited interaction is allowed by their experimental design 'in the sense that participants made one-time decisions based on the prior decisions of others' (2009, p. 461) and one could argue that the decision making process is a much more complicated procedure in terms of real networks of people that exist outside an experimental environment.[6] Even inside their experimental worlds, one could hypothesise that one could easily develop forms of interaction that the researchers may not have been aware of or able to avoid. For example, no one could guarantee that each participant listened to the songs alone. Our purpose is to build on Salganik and Watts' experiments by adopting main features from their design and modifying the procedure, so as to be able to chart the mechanics of influence which may develop as part of the sociality indigenous and specific to particular networked environments.

A proposed method for deconstructing musical preference

Following the evaluation of Salganik and Watts' experiment, we propose an experimental plan which aims to deconstruct and analyse the 'microphysics' of different types of social influences on the decision making process associated with the choice of musical products (as typical representatives of the class of credence goods), using several aspects of social networking analysis. Salganik and Watts' experiment (2009) aimed to analyse the decision making process within multiple worlds of independent and socially influenced (or dependent) circumstances. We propose that socially influenced conditions must be analysed further, by using participants who have been previously acquainted in order to observe the effect interpersonal relationships have on the results.

More specifically, our intention is to attempt to incorporate a musical experiment into several small networks of people whose relationships and personal ties, as well as the strength of their ties, will be previously charted and represented in sociometric graphs. The networks of participants will have previously been acquainted; however, during the laboratory study no contact will be allowed. Providing this 'sterile' environment secures the data collection process from an undesirable and uncountable flow of influence among participants who will only be informed of the average rating of each song and the preferences of other voters. They will then be able to change their votes before the end of the whole procedure, allowing the experimenters to gauge the degree of influence already charted hubs may have had on participants' final decisions. Similarly, music business intermediaries' influence (such as DJs, music TV presenters and critics) will also be made known during the experiment, in order to observe their effect on participants' final decision. These two experimental conditions aim to investigate whether the final choices made by participants will be the result of influence resulting from previously existing networked relationships or from the music business intermediary's stated song preferences, allowing us, therefore, to assess the rate of influence of central nodes in the network of participants and compare it to the influence exerted by expert opinion of the industry, as operationalised by the choices of business intermediaries. This way, our experiment attempts to investigate the tie-to-tie trust, vis-a-vis the influence of the established authority of cultural professionals.

Our hypotheses are as follows: (a) that the ties developed within particular networks of relationships will be significant in the formation of musical tastes (operationalised for the purposes of this experiment as song ratings); (b) that knowledge of musical intermediaries tastes will also act as a discernible influence; and (c) that this influence will, however, be less significant than the one afforded by the ties which are indigenous to pre-established networks of interpersonal relationships. In other words, participants who are central nodes within each network are expected to lead the herd behaviour (Brown et al., 1987), while interpersonal binary relationships are expected to have similar voting behaviours. On the basis of observations in recent word-of-mouth research (Trusov et al., 2009), which argue that in the Web 2.0 people are more apt to be influenced by consumer rather than expert recommendations, our main hypothesis is that the influence of official intermediaries will be less significant than that of the central nodes already in existence within a network. Therefore, the experiment described will enable us and other researchers to test the hypothesis that the Web 2.0 will shift the advice-seeking processes to more personal ties compared with that of firm-initiated information.[7]

Conclusion

Regardless of the limitations of and consequent objections to the use of experiments in cultural research, we, nevertheless feel, that the experimental condition we propose can provide a useful starting point for the investigation of network dynamics. These may then, at a later stage, be counterposed with rich data resulting from the investigation and thick description of these issues through the use of other methods of social research, which will provide more in-depth analyses of the context and background of the observed network dynamics.

The central conceptual questions that have prompted this method of experimentation arise from scepticism towards the applicability of hierarchical models of influence developed during the course of the twentieth century for the analysis of complex, and potentially horizontal, relations of influence which may be indigenous to the contemporary social networks developing in the ecology of the Web 2.0. Our experimental design aims at charting these potentially novel forms of influence and assessing them in comparison with both the power of influence which established cultural intermediaries have been traditionally thought to possess and the established commonsensical assumptions concerning the naturalness or inevitability of taste characteristic of everyday cultural consumption.

This way, the applicability of the two-step flow theory of influence for contemporary networked environments in the very unpredictable field of music will be empirically tested, a test which will be of interest not only within the limits of academic debate on cultural taste and consumption but also for professionals in the music industry, who can potentially acquire a better understanding of the mechanics of development of contemporary musical tastes.

Notes

1. For a recent review on the continuing battle of the music industry against forms of distribution and consumption resulting from peer-to-peer practices, see Cammaerts (2011).

2. We have to note however that recent studies have shown that consumers are not keen on admitting failure to discern quality in products or services (see Nakayama *et al.*, 2010).
3. The last decade has seen the development of a rich literature within the fields of cultural sociology, media and cultural studies and production studies, investigating whether the notion of cultural intermediaries originally put forward by Bourdieu (1984) retains its original explanatory power (Nixon & Du Gay, 2002; Maguire & Matthews, 2010), the function of cultural intermediaries within various sectors of the cultural industries (see Negus, 2002, on the music industry and Wright, 2005, on publishing), and, more recently, discussing the ways in which the expansion of cultural industries together with the abundance of cultural goods brought about by the new forms of distribution and consequent cultural networks may be destabilizing the power of traditional cultural intermediaries (Wright, 2011).
4. According to the Nielsen Company, global consumers spent more than five and half hours on social networking sites like Facebook and Twitter in December 2009, an 82% increase from the same time last year, when users were spending just over three hours on social networking sites. In addition, the overall traffic to social networking sites has grown over the last three years. (Nielsen Wire, 2010).
5. For an extensive review of the notion of homophily, see McPherson *et al.* (2001).
6. To this end, Bakshy *et al.* (2011), turn to the investigation of the diffusion rate of Twitter microblogging posts, arguing that that word-of-mouth information spreads via many small cascades, mostly triggered by ordinary individuals and not highly visible public figures like media representatives, celebrities, and government officials.
7. 'The outcomes of the interpersonal exchanges are provision of, and/or access to, consumption-related information that holds some "informational value" over and above the formal advertising messages provided by the company and that holds influence over the individual's decision making' (Brown *et al.*, 2007, p. 4).

References

Adorno, T. (1991) Culture industry reconsidered, in: J. M. Bernstein (Ed.) *The culture industry: selected essays on mass culture* (London, Routledge), 98–106.
Afuah, A. & Tucci, C. (2001) *Internet business models and strategies* (Boston, MA, McGraw Hill).

Arthur, B. W. (1996) Increasing returns and the new world of business, *Harvard Business Review*, 100–109.
Bakshy, E., Hofman, J. M., Mason, W. A. & Watts, D. J. (2011) Everyone's an influencer: quantifying influence on twitter, *Proceedings of the fourth ACM International Conference on Web Search and Data Mining*, 65–74.
Barabasi, A. (2002) *Linked, the new science of networks* (New York, Perseus Books).
Blackburn, D. (2004) On-line piracy and recorded music sales, *Ariel*, 2, 1–42.
Bourdieu, P. (1984) *Distinction: a social critique of the judgement of taste* (London, Routledge & Kegan Paul).
Brown, J. J. & Reingen, P. H. (1987) Social ties and word-of-mouth referral behavior, *The Journal of Consumer Research*, 14(3), 350–362.
Brown, J., Broderick, A. J. & Lee, N. (2007) Word of mouth communication within online communities: conceptualizing the online social network, *Journal of Interactive Marketing*, 21(3), 2–20.
Cammaerts, B. (2011) The hegemonic copyright regime vs the sharing copyright users of music? *Media, Culture & Society*, 33(3), 491–502.
Caves, R. E. (2000) *Creative industries: contracts between arts and commerce* (Cambridge, MA, Harvard University Press).
Coleman, J. S., Katz, E. & Menzel, H. (1957) The diffusion of an innovation among physicians, *Sociometry*, 20, 253–270.
Cunningham, S. (2004) The creative industries after cultural policy: a genealogy and some possible preferred futures, *International Journal of Cultural Studies*, 7, 105–115.
Davis, A., Gardner, B. B. & Gardner, M. R. (1941) *Deep south* (Chicago, IL, University of Chicago Press).
DCMS (Department for Culture, Media and Sport) (1998) *Creative industries mapping document*, Creative Task Force. London, U.K. Government, Department for Culture, Media and Sports.
du Gay, P. & Pryke, M (Eds) (2002) *Cultural economy: cultural analysis and commercial life* (London, Sage).
Earls, M. (2007) *Herd: how to change mass behaviour by harnessing our true nature* (Chichester, UK, John Wiley & Sons).
Emons, W. (1997) Credence goods and fraudulent experts, *Rand Journal of Economics*, 28(1), 107–119.
Frank, R. H. & Cook, P. J. (1995) *The winner-take-all society* (New York, The Free Press).
Freestone, O. & Mitchell, V. W. (2004) Generation Y attitudes towards e-ethics and internet-related misbehaviours, *Journal of Business Ethics*, 54, 121–128.
Friedkin, N. (1980) A test of structural features of Granovetter's strength of weak ties theory, *Social Networks*, 2, 411–422.
Granovetter, M. (1974) *Getting a job* (Cambridge, MA, Harvard University Press).
Hax, A. & Wilde III, D. L. (2001) *The Delta Model: discovering new sources of profitability in a networked economy* (New York, Palgrave).
Homans, G. G. (1950) *The human group* (New York, Harcourt, Brace).
Katz, E. (2001) Lazarsfeld's map of media effects, *International Journal of Public Opinion Research*, 13(3), 270–279.
Katz, E. (2009 (1955)) Lazarsfeld's legacy: the power of limited effects. Introduction to the transaction edition, in: E. Katz & P. F. Lazarsfeld (Eds) *Personal influence: the part played by people in the flow of mass communications* (New Brunswick, NJ, Transaction Publishers).
Katz, E. & Lazarsfeld, P. F. (2009 (1955)) *Personal influence: the part played by people in the flow of mass communications* (New Brunswick, NJ, Transaction Publishers).
Katz, M. L. & Shapiro, C. (1985) Network externalities, competition and compatibility, *American Economic Review*, 75, 424–440.
Klimis, G. M. & Wallis, R. (2009) Copyright and entrepreneurship: catalyst or barrier? *Information, Communication and Society*, 12(2), 267–286.
Kretschmer, M., Klimis, G. M. & Choi, C. J. (1999) Increasing returns and social contagion in cultural industries, *British Journal of Management*, 10, S61–S72.
Kretschmer, M., Klimis, G. M. & Wallis, R. (2001) Music in electronic markets: an empirical study, *New Media & Society*, 3(4), 417–441.
Lazarsfeld, P. F., Berelson, B. & Gaudet, H. (1944) *The people's choice: how the voter makes up his mind in a presidential campaign* (New York, Duell, Sloan & Pearce).
Liebowitz, S. (2005) File-sharing: creative destruction or just plain destruction? *Journal of Law and Economics*, (XLIX), 1–28.
Maguire, J. S. & Matthews, J. (2010) Cultural intermediaries and the media, *Sociology Compass*, 4(7), 405–416.
McPherson, M., Smith-Lovin, L. & Cook, J. M. (2001) Birds of a feather: homophily in social networks, *Annual Review of Sociology*, 27(1), 415–444.
Nakayama, M., Sutcliffe, N. & Wan, Y. (2010) Has the web transformed experience goods into search goods? *Electronic Markets*, 20(3–4), 251–262.
Negus, K. (2002) The work of cultural intermediaries and the enduring distance between production and consumption, *Cultural Studies*, 16(4), 501–515.
Nielsen Wire (2010) Led by Facebook, Twitter, global time spent on social media sites up 82% year over year. Available online at: <http://blog.nielsen.com/nielsenwire/global/led-by-facebook-twitter-global-time-spent-on-social-media-sites-up-82-year-over-year/>

Nixon, S. & Du Gay, P. (2002) Who needs cultural intermediaries? *Cultural Studies*, 16(4), 495–500.

Oberholzer-Gee F. & Strumpf K. (2007) The Effect of File Sharing on Record Sales: An Empirical Analysis, *Journal of Political Economy*, 115(1), 1–42.

Ortiz-Arroyo, D. (2010) Discovering sets of key players in social networks, in: Ab. Ajith, Ab. E. Hassanien & V. Snášel (Eds) *Computational social network analysis trends, tools and research advances* (London, Springer-Verlag), 27–47.

Petroczi, A., Bazsó, F. & Nepusz, T. (2006) Measuring tie-strength in virtual social networks, *Connections*, 27(2), 39–52.

Porter, M. (2001) Strategy and the Internet, *Harvard Business Review*, 79(3), 62–78.

Potts, J., Cunningham, St., Hartley, J. & Ormerod, P. (2008) Social network markets: a new definition of the creative industries, *Journal of Cultural Economics*, 32(3), 167–185.

Rogers, E. M. (2003) *Diffusion of innovations*, (5th edn) (New York, Free Press).

Salganik, M. J. & Watts, D. J. (2009) Web-based experiments for the study of collective social dynamics in cultural markets, *Topics in Cognitive Science*, 1(3), 439–468.

Salganik, M. J, Watts, D.J, & Dodds, P. S. (2006) Experimental study of inequality and unpredictability in an artificial cultural market, *Science*, 311(5762), 854–856.

Schumpeter, J. (1950) *Capitalism, Socialism and Democracy* (New York, Harper & Row).

Schumpeter, J. (1934) *Theory of economic development: An inquiry into the business cycle* (Cambridge, MA: Harvard University Press).

Smith, D., Menon, S. & Sivakumar, K. (2005) Online peer and editorial recommendations, trust, and choice in virtual markets, *Journal of Interactive Marketing*, 19(3), 15–37.

Tapscott, D. (1996) *The digital economy: promise and peril in the age of networked intelligence* (New York, McGraw-Hill).

Tapscott, M., Bucklin, E. & Pauwels, K. (2009) Effects of word of mouth versus traditional marketing: Finding from an Internet Networking site, *American Marketing Association*, 73, 90–102.

Trusov M., Bucklin E. & Pauwels K. (2009) Effects of word of Mouth versus traditional marketing: Finding from an Internet Networking site, *American Marketing Association*, 73, 90–102.

Watts, D. J. & Strogatz, S. H. (1998) Collective dynamics of 'small-world' networks, *Nature*, 393(6684), 440–442.

Whyte Jr, W. H. (1954) The web of word of mouth, *Fortune*, 50, 140–143.

Wright, D. (2005) Mediating production and consumption: cultural capital and 'cultural workers', *The British Journal of Sociology*, 56(1), 105–121.

Wright, D. (2011) Making tastes for everything: omnivorousness and cultural abundance, *Journal for Cultural Research*, 15(4), 355–371.

Zhang, M. (2010) Social network analysis: history, concepts, and research, in: B. Furht (Ed.) *Handbook of social network technologies and applications* (New York, Springer), 3–21.

Index

Acquisti, A. 92
activism 12–13
Adorno, T. 105
advertising 75, 77, 93; personalised 77
Afuah, A. 104
agency *see* social intermediaries and location of agency
agent-based computer simulations: Web 1.0 vs Web 2.0 7–12
Albrechtslund, A. 32
Alevizou, P. 38
Alexander, B. 38
Alexander, C.J. 53
Allen, M. 92
amateur users 76–8
Amazon 75
The American Prospect 7
analytical framework *see* framework for analysis of Web 2.0 interactivity
Andarson, J. 24
Anderson, C. 75, 77
Andrejevic, M. 91, 92, 93, 95
'Arab Spring' 25, 52, 54
Arthur, B.W. 106
artists 17, 20–1; deviantART 32, 37, 38, 39–42, 43–7; *see also* music
asymmetrical power relations 95
Axelrod, R. 8
Axtell, R. 8

Bagdikian, B. 25
Bainbridge, W.S. 5
banking 104
Barabási, A.-L. 3, 9, 23, 107
Bauwens, M. 74, 76, 77, 78, 79, 80, 81, 82
Beer, D. 6, 31, 90, 91, 93, 95
Belgium 38; PloneGov 65
Benedikt, M. 94
Benkler, Y. 73, 74, 75, 79–80, 84–5
Berg, B.L. 40
Bessen, J. 80
Bimber, B.A. 54
BIND 73, 75

Bird, E.S. 91
Blackburn, D. 105
blogs 6–7, 18–19, 24; linking 20
Bohman, J. 53
Boldrin, M. 80
Bordewijk, J.L. 46
Bourdieu, P. 106
Boyd, D.M. 4, 23, 91
Boyle, P. 19, 20
Brabham, D.C. 54
Breslin, J.G. 38
Brin, S. 77
Brissett, D. 46
Brown, J. 110
Brown, J.J. 114
Bruns, A. 74, 81–2
Burrell, R. 80
Burrows, R. 6, 90, 91, 93, 95
Butterfield, Stewart 38
'butterfly effect' 11

Caldas, A. 54
capitalism 95
Castells, M. 54, 56, 90
Caves, R.E. 105
Chadwick, A. 54, 56
Chakravarty, S. 79
chaotic systems 5
Christodoulou, S.P. 38
citizen consultation and citizen sourcing of expertise 52, 67–9; co-creating 56, 57–8, 59, 62–3, 68; contributing 56, 57, 58, 59, 62–3, 68; Dutton's taxonomy 56–8; empowerment 52, 53; EU policies 52–6; limitations of the study 69–70; real-time chat 68; research methodology 58–62; results 62–7; sharing 56–7, 58, 59, 62–3, 68–9; transparency 52, 66, 67
citizen-journalists 7
citizenship, digital 2, 3
cliques 107, 108, 110
Cobo, R.C. 52
Coffin, J. 81, 82
Cohen, P. 21

INDEX

Coleman, A. 80
Coleman, J.S. 109
collaborative network organisations (CNOs) 55, 56–8
commons, digital knowledge 15–17, 21–3, 27; form and meaning: hunger for reality 17–18; information sampling and linking 19–21; new realities – new kinds of hunger 24–7; researching new realities 23–4; Web 2.0 and information revolution 18–19
Commons-based platforms 73–4, 75–6, 78–85
computer simulations: Web 1.0 vs Web 2.0 7–12
Conole, G. 38
contagion 109
Cook, P.J. 106
copyright 17, 19, 20, 80, 104
Corbin, J.M. 39
corporate monitoring, storing and processing of data 95
corporate news producers 25
corporate world: legitimacy and authority 22
corporatization 32
Couldry, N. 96
Cox, A. 38
Crawford, C. 33
Creative Commons or General Public Licenses 78, 81
creative destruction 104
crowdsourcing 54, 56, 75, 77–8
cultural industries 104–6; herd behaviour 106; measuring inequality in unpredictable cultural markets: contemporary experiments 111–12; proposed method for deconstructing musical preference 113–14; web experimental network design after Salganik and Watts 112–13; *see also* artists
Cunningham, S. 105
Curran, J. 46

David, P.A. 62
Davis, A. 107
De Marez, L. 38, 39
de Zúñiga, H.G. 25
Dean, J. 95
Debatin, B. 92
definition of Web 2.0 1–2
democracy 23–4, 25, 26, 27, 46, 47, 54–5, 94; *see also* citizen consultation and citizen sourcing of expertise
den Besten, M. 84
Denton Jr, R.E. 26
DesignCrowd 78
desktop manufacturing 85
Deuze, M. 12
deviantART 32, 37, 38, 39–42, 43–7
Dewitt, L. 24
dictatorship, benevolent 82, 84

diffusion 109, 110
'digital natives' 24, 27
do-it-yourself (DIY) culture 85
Downes, E. 32, 33
du Gay, P. 105
Dutton, W.H. 54–5, 56, 57, 58, 62, 68
Dwyer, C. 92

Earls, M. 106
Easley, D. 52, 53
eBay 75
eGovernment Awards, European 60–1
Egypt 54
Ellison, N. 4, 23, 89, 91
Emons, W. 105
empowerment 25, 52, 53, 61, 94
entrepreneurship 104
Epstein, J. 8
equipotentiality 82, 83
Erdos, Paul 107
ethics 77
Etzioni, A. 52
European Union: citizen consultation and citizen sourcing of expertise *see separate entry*

Facebook 2, 19, 21, 22, 23, 52, 75, 77, 78, 91; civic participation 54, 64, 66, 67–8, 69
Fake, Caterina 38
fiction and nonfiction 17
Finen, T. 24
Fischer, Maria 20–1
Flickr 32, 37–8, 39–47, 64, 75, 77, 78
Fontana, A. 40
framework for analysis of Web 2.0 interactivity 31–2, 46–7; application of 37–41; definition of affordances 34; document affordances 34, 36, 43–4; functional affordances 35–7; interactivity concept 32–3; results and discussion 41–5; structural affordances 33–5, 36–7; user affordances 34, 36, 42–3; website affordances 34, 36, 44–5
Frank, R.H. 106
Free Software Foundation 79, 80–1
free speech 80
free/open source software (FOSS) 20, 57, 75, 78, 79, 82, 85
Freeman, J. 83
Freemium model 75, 77
Frey, J. 17, 40
Friedkin, N. 8, 108
Fuchs, C. 1–2, 13, 93, 95

G2C (government-to-citizen) interactions *see* citizen consultation and citizen sourcing of expertise
Gasser, U. 27
Gauntlett, D. 90

120

INDEX

Gehl, R.W. 93, 94, 95
General Public or Creative Commons Licenses 78, 81
Germany: Buergerhaushalt 67
Ghosh, R. 79
Gibson, R.K. 54, 56
Gibson-Graham, J.K. 27
Giddens, A. 92
Giglietto, F. 3
globalisation 26
Golder, S.A. 37
González-Bailón, S. 52, 53
Goodwin, A. 19
Google 75, 77, 80–1
governments: citizen consultation and citizen sourcing of expertise *see separate entry*
Granovetter, M. 108, 110
Greece 7; Ermis 66–7
Gross, R. 92

hackers 76–7, 78
Hagström, M. 55, 68
Hammond, T. 37
Hardy, C. 53–4
Hax, A. 104
Hendricks, J.A. 26
herd behaviour 106
Hermans, L. 24, 25
heterarchies 81–2, 83, 84
Hilbert, M. 83
Hindman, M. 53–4
Hoegg, R. 31, 32
Hoem, J. 46
Hoeschele, W. 83–4
Hogan, B.J. 34, 35
holoptism 83
Homans, George Gaspar 107
homophily 110
Hood, C.C. 52, 54
Howe, J. 75, 78
Huberman, A. 37, 40
Hudson-Smith, A. 32
human rights 81; free speech 80
hunger for reality *see* sampling and linking information
Hwang, W.-Y. 35–6

individual-oriented agency *see* social intermediaries and location of agency
influence, social 108–14
information production in the Social Web, political economy of 73–6; Commons-based platforms 73–4, 75–6, 78–85; proprietary-based platforms 73–4, 75, 76–8, 84
InnoCentive 52, 78
innovations: diffusion of 109, 110; intellectual property and 80–1

instrumental and institutional views *see* social intermediaries and location of agency
insurance 104
integrity, personal 92
intellectual property (IP) 80–1; copyright 17, 19, 20, 80, 104
interactivity concept 32–3, 92
iStockphoto 78

Jakobsson, P. 32
Jaokar, A. 32
Jarkoff, Scott 38
Jarrett, K. 32, 92, 98
Jenkins, H. 90
Jensen, J.F. 32–3
Jensen, M.J. 25
Jurgenson, N. 2, 91

Kahn, R. 2
Katerelos, I. 9
Katz, E. 108, 109
Katz, M.L. 106
Keen, A. 6
Kellner, D. 2
Kincaid, J. 91
Kiousis, S. 33
Kishida, K. 82
Kleinberg, J. 52, 53
Kleiner, D. 76
Klimis, G.M. 105
knowledge commons, digital 15–17, 21–3, 27; form and meaning: hunger for reality 17–18; information sampling and linking 19–21; new realities – new kinds of hunger 24–7; researching new realities 23–4; Web 2.0 and information revolution 18–19
Kostakis, V. 75, 76, 77, 78, 79, 80, 81, 82, 83, 84
Kretschmer, M. 105, 111

Laisne, J. 79
Lakhani, K. 79
Lampe, C. 91
Lan, Z.G. 53
Laurent, O. 38
Lazarsfeld, P.F. 108, 109
Lazer, D. 5
Leiner, D.J. 33
Lessig, L. 80, 81
Lethem, J. 19–20
Levine, D. 80
Levy, S. 76
Lewins, A. 40
Licklider, J.C.R. 3
Liebowitz, S. 104–5
Lilleker, D.G. 33
LinkedIn 52, 64

INDEX

linking *see* sampling and linking information
Linux 20, 82
Lipp, J. 24
lock-in 106
Lorenz, E.N. 11
Loubser, M. 84

Mackay, J.B. 18
McKenna, K.Y.A. 91
McKibben, B. 21, 26
McLeod, K. 80
McMillan, S.J. 32, 33
McNeal, R.S. 53
McStay, A. 95
Malagon, C. 33
Malcolm, J. 82
Maness, J.M. 38
Margetts, H.Z. 52, 54
Marshall, M.N. 39
Marx, K. 74, 75, 76
mash-ups 19
mass media 106
Mayo, E. 107
Mead, G.H. 92
memoir 17
Menzies, H. 19
meritocracy 81–2
Meuer, M. 80
Microsoft 75
Miles, M. 40
Milgram, S. 10, 22, 107
Miller, P. 38
mobility, virtual 26
Monge, P. 24
Moreno, Jacob Levy 107
Morrison, B. 17
Morse, J. 39
Mozilla Firefox browser 73, 75
multi-agent computer simulations: Web 1.0 vs Web 2.0 7–12
music 104; forces shaping musical taste 109, 111–14; from experts to networks in music industry 106; P2P file sharing 104–5; sampling 19
MySpace 75; civic participation 54

Nakakoji, K. 82
Nardi, B.A. 36
nation-states 22
neoliberalism 92, 96
The New Republic 7
New York Times 7
Newhagen, J.E. 33
Newman, M.E.J. 53
news from Internet 21, 25; aggregators 18, 20
newspapers 7, 18, 21, 25
99designs 78

nonfiction and fiction 17
Norman, D. 34

Oberholzer-Gee, F. 105
oil, peak 26
Oldenburg, R. 46
O'Neil, M. 83
onion model 82
open design movement 85
open source software/FOSS 20, 57, 75, 78, 79, 82, 85
opinion leaders 108–9
O'Reilly, T. 1, 32, 38, 75, 94
Ortiz-Arroyo, D. 110

Page, L. 77
Pal, L.A. 53
Palfrey, J. 27
Papacharissi, Z. 51
Pardo, K.H. 52
Parenti, M. 25
Pariser, E. 18, 77
pastiche 17, 19
patents 80
Patmore, C. 39
Patry, W. 80
Patton, M.Q. 39
peak oil 26
peer, public and private property 81
Peitgen, H.-O. 9
Pelzer, B. 91
Perez, C. 85
personal integrity 92
Petersen, S.M. 32, 95
Petroczi, A. 106
photographs 20, 23; Flickr 32, 37–8, 39–47, 64, 75, 77, 78; iStockphoto 78; mash-ups 19
Pissard, N. 38
plagiarism 17, 19–20
political blogging 7
political economy of information production in the Social Web 73–6; Commons-based platforms 73–4, 75–6, 78–85; proprietary-based platforms 73–4, 75, 76–8, 84
Ponte, L.M. 19
pornography 77
Porter, J. 75, 76
Porter, M. 104
Potts, J. 105
power relations, asymmetrical 95
Prieur, C. 38
privacy 69, 77, 84, 92
produser 91
profit maximisation and profit generation 79
proprietary-based platforms 73–4, 75, 76–8, 84

122

INDEX

prosumption culture/prosumer 2, 7, 91; *see also* framework for analysis of Web 2.0 interactivity; sampling and linking information
protest 12–13
Pryke, M. 105
public, private and peer property 81
public sector: citizen consultation and citizen sourcing of expertise *see separate entry*
Putnam, R. 22–3, 24, 26
Pyyhtinen, O. 97, 98

Quiring, O. 33

radio 7, 18
Rafaeli, S. 32
Rainie, L. 24
Raymond, E. 82, 84
reality hunger *see* sampling and linking information
Reid, D. 35
Reid, F. 35
Renyi, Alfred 107
Rheingold, H. 3, 94
Rigby, B. 38
Ritzer, G. 2, 91
Rogers, E.M. 109, 110
Rosadiuk, A. 39
Rossi, L. 3
Rushkoff, D. 78

Salganik, M.J. 111, 112–13
sampling and linking information 15–17, 19–21, 27; form and meaning: hunger for reality 17–18; new digital knowledge commons 21–3; new realities – new kinds of hunger 24–7; researching new realities 23–4; Web 2.0 and information revolution 18–19
Sassen, S. 20, 21, 26
scarcity 83–4, 85
Scholz, T. 6, 32, 94
Schor, J.B. 20, 21, 22
Schumate, M. 24
Schumpeter, J. 104
Schuurman, D. 38, 39
scientific research 5
Sendmail 73–4, 75
Shapiro, C. 106
sharing/aggregation economies 77, 78
Shields, D. 16–18, 19, 20, 27
shipping 104
Shirky, C. 90
Silver, C. 40
Silver, D. 94
Simmel, G. 92, 97–8
simulating Web 1.0 vs Web 2.0 7–12
six degrees of separation 107–8
Skocpol, T. 26

small-world network 9–10
Smith, D. 111
social capital 22–3, 54, 56, 67
social construction of knowledge 27
social influence 108–14
social intermediaries and location of agency 89–90, 98–9; egocentric networks and individual-oriented agency 90–3; labour under siege and system-oriented agency 93–5; towards reconfigured conceptual apparatus 96–8
social network analysis (SNA): analytical tools used in 110–11; conceptual roots of 106–8; measuring inequality in unpredictable cultural markets: contemporary experiments 111–12; mechanics of influence 108–9; proposed method for deconstructing musical preference 113–14; web experimental network design after Salganik and Watts 112–13
social simulations: Web 1.0 vs Web 2.0 7–12
Solop, F.I. 25, 26
Sotira, Angelo 38, 39
Soukup, C. 46
Spain: eCatalunya 64, 69; Participa en Andalucía 65–6
Sprott, J.C. 9
Stadler, F. 82
Stephens, Matt 38
Stephenson, K. 81
Stern, A. 32
Stiernstedt, F. 32
Strauss, A.L. 39
strength-of-weak ties 108, 110
Strogatz, S. 9
Strumpf, K. 105
Stutzman, F. 92
Styliaras, G.D. 38
Sunstein, C.R. 26
surveillance, electronic 32, 84, 95
system-oriented agency *see* social intermediaries and location of agency
Szuprowicz, B. 33

Tapscott, D. 1
Tapscott, M. 104
Taylor, R.W. 3
television 6, 18, 21, 25
Tenopir, C. 6
Terranova, T. 95
third places, virtual 46, 47
three-dimensional (3D) printing 85
Thrift, N. 95
Thurow, Lester 104
Toffler, A. 91
Tolbert, C.J. 53
Torvalds, Linus 82
Toscan, C. 33
transportation costs 26

INDEX

Tremayne, M. 33
Trusov, M. 114
trust in communities 25
Tsekeris, C. 6, 7, 8
Tucci, C. 104
Tunisia 54
Turkle, S. 94
Twitter 6, 19, 22, 52, 64, 66, 67–8, 69

Urry, J. 5

Valafar, M. 38
Valenzuela, S. 91
Van Abel, B. 85
Van Dijk, J. 53–4
van Kaam, B. 46
Vergeer, M. 24, 25, 91
Vespignani, A. 5
voluntarism 79

Wakabayashi, C. 32
Waldman, S. 25
Wales, Jimmy 82
Wall Street Journal 7
Wallis, R. 105
Wark, M. 76
Warner, L. 107
Watts, D.J. 21, 23, 108, 111, 112–13

Web 1.0 2, 18; simulating Web 2.0 vs 7–12
Web 3.0 2
Web 4.0 2
Weber, M.S. 24
Weber, S. 84
Wikimedia Foundation 79, 80–1
Wikipedia 2, 20, 52, 57, 75, 78, 79, 81, 82, 83, 85
Wilde III, D.L. 104
Williams, A.D. 1
Winfrey, Oprah 17
Wolf, R. 79
Wonders, B.J. 26
Wyrick, B. 76

Yang, L. 53
Ye, Y. 82
YouTube 2, 52, 75, 77, 78; civic participation 54, 64

Zeldich, M. 111
Zhang, M. 107, 108, 110–11
Zhang, W. 54
Zimmer, M. 32, 93, 94
Zite 18